CONTROVERSY!

Steroids

Jon Sterngass

Marshall Cavendish
Benchmark
New York

With thanks to John M. Roll, Professor and Associate Dean for Research and Director of the Program of Excellence in the Addictions at Washington State University College of Nursing

Library of Congress Cataloging-in-Publication Data
Sterngass, Jon • Steroids / Jon Sterngass.
p. cm. —(Controversy!) • Includes bibliographical references and index.
ISBN 978-0-7614-4903-4
1. Anabolic steroids—Juvenile literature. I. Title. • RC1230.S725 2011
362.29—dc22 • 2009033406

Publisher: Michelle Bisson • Art Director: Anahid Hamparian
Series Designer: Alicia Mikles • Photo research by Lindsay Aveilhe

The photographs in this book are used by permission and through the courtesy of:
iStockphoto.com/Steve Goodwin: cover; Hiroko Masuike/Getty Images: 4; Andrew Holbrooke/ Corbis: 8; Matt Sullivan/Reuters: 11; AP Photo/DEA: 18; Darryl Estrine/Getty Images: 21; AP Photo/LM Otero, File: 31; Popperfoto/Getty Images: 36; AFP/Getty Images: 41, 44; Felix R. Cid/Redux: 51; The Granger Collection: 59; Milk Photographie/Corbis: 64; Dr. Jurgen Scriba/Photo Researchers, Inc.: 73; AP Photo/Enid News & Eagle, Andy Carpenean: 75; Chris Pizzello/Reuters: 81; Barton Silverman/The New York Times/ Redux: 87; Clive Mason/Getty Images: 93; Newscom: 100; Olivier Morin/AFP /Getty Images: 104; Win McNamee/Getty Images: 107; David Silverman/Getty Images: 111.

Printed in Malaysia (T)
1 3 5 6 4 2

Contents

Marion Jones was not only stripped of her five Olympic gold medals as a result of her steroid use, but served six months in prison for lying under oath. For a time, she became a public symbol of the evils of steroid use.

1 The Controversy over Anabolic Steroids

Steroids Scandal

In the late 1990s, Marion Jones was a female American track and field superstar. In 1998, Jones achieved the amazing feat of winning every race in which she competed. She was the first woman in fifty years to win the one hundred meters, two hundred meters, and long jump, becoming U.S. champion in all three. That year alone, Jones earned about $7 million from endorsements.

In the 2000 Summer Olympics in Australia, Jones gave the greatest performance by a woman track athlete in Olympic history. She won an astonishing five medals—three of them gold—including the one hundred/two hundred double and the long jump. She won the one hundred by .37 seconds, the widest margin since the Olympics began using electronic timing in 1968.

Marion Jones returned to the United States as an Olympic hero. She was featured on the covers of *Vogue, Time, Newsweek,* and *Sports Illustrated for Women.* Jones had gained millions of new fans from the television coverage of the Summer Games. She was in great demand by advertisers and had a multimillion-dollar endorsement deal with Nike. Jones finished the 2001 season ranked #1 in the world in both the one hundred and the two hundred.

Jones's time of triumph, however, was short-lived. In 2003, the U.S. government issued a search warrant for the Bay Area Laboratory Co-Operative (BALCO), a California business that specialized in blood and urine analysis and food supplements.

The search uncovered records of purchases, doping calendars, and various blood-test results connected to many professional athletes, including Jones and her former coach. BALCO founder Victor Conte repeatedly accused Jones of using performance-enhancing drugs and said he watched her inject herself with steroids.

In 2004, Jones sued Victor Conte for $25 million for defamation of character. She claimed Conte's lies hurt her reputation and cost her endorsement money. Under oath before a grand jury, and in many public statements throughout her career, Jones insisted that she never used anabolic steroids or any performance-enhancing drugs. "I'm drug-free, always have been and always will be," she said in 2004.

In fact, between 2000 and 2007, Jones had used a number of undetectable performance-enhancing substances such as human growth hormone, insulin, and the endurance booster EPO. She was also using "The Clear," an anabolic steroid administered by placing a couple of drops under the tongue. In those years, she had been tested more than twenty times and not a single test had come back positive for performance-enhancing drugs.

In 2007, Jones publicly admitted her past steroid use and retired from track and field. She confessed to doping "several times before the Sydney Olympics and continued using it after." Jones returned all five of her Olympic medals and in 2008, she served six months in federal prison for lying under oath to two grand juries about her personal use of anabolic steroids.

In seven years, the use of steroids had transformed Marion Jones from a world record holder and American hero into, as one sporting official called her, "one of the biggest frauds in sporting history."

Controversy

Anabolic steroids are synthetic substances related to naturally produced male sex hormones such as testosterone. Steroids imitate testosterone's effects. In the United States, doctors prescribe steroids for a variety of medical conditions. However, perhaps as many as a million Americans of all ages use steroids to improve their looks or boost athletic performance.

This latter use of steroids makes them controversial. In 1991 the U.S. government listed anabolic steroids as a Schedule III controlled substance. This makes the possession of steroids without a prescription a federal crime punishable by up to seven years in prison. Users of steroids for nontherapeutic reasons act in violation of federal law and the rules of all sports federations.

Nonetheless, people keep using them. Anabolic steroids produce increases in strength and allow a person to train longer and harder. Anabolic steroid use, combined with weight training and adequate dietary protein intake, can build muscle mass and strength beyond weight training alone. Negative short-term side effects of steroid use seem to be reversible, although long-term, high-dose effects are largely unknown. However, many adults, whether professional athletes or not, view anabolic steroids and their possible negative side effects as a fair trade-off for better looks or improved performance in sports. These people take steroids the same way they would use the best diet or the best training techniques.

This would be a short book if the only issue regarding anabolic steroids and other performance-enhancing substances was their legality. In the United States, they are not legal for nontherapeutic reasons. On that level, there is nothing more to write. The use of steroids is against the rules and this is cheating. The more interesting philosophical question, however, is whether the laws and rules should be changed to allow the use of anabolic steroids.

General Use of Anabolic Steroids

Traditionally, the use of anabolic steroids has been seen as an issue affecting elite athletics. The media's depiction of steroids usually involves major sporting events such as the Olympics or occasions

Many steroid users are teenagers, some of whom get the idea to use steroids as children wanting to be strong like their built-up, muscular dads.

when sportspeople have tested positive for a banned substance. However, steroid use is not restricted to athletes. Most Americans who have used steroids are not looking to set a new world's record but simply to look and feel better. Many steroid users are adolescents under the age of eighteen, and this raises a host of different issues.

The controversy over nonathletes who take steroids shares many similarities with the general debate over the legality of drugs in the United States. First, there is the medical question: how dangerous are steroids? Hundreds of studies have attempted to answer this question, yet their results have varied widely. Whether dangerous or not, there is the larger philosophical question of the proper role of government in people's personal lives. Should the U.S. government restrict the choices of informed and consenting adults who want to use anabolic steroids for cosmetic reasons? Many Americans already abuse dangerous substances such as alcohol and tobacco in their daily lives. If these are legal without a prescription, why not anabolic steroids?

Finally, there are questions involved in the practical aspects of drug testing for steroids. How accurate is drug testing? Is mandatory drug testing for workers and students a violation of privacy? How can workers or students who are accused of steroid use be guaranteed due process?

Steroids and Elite Sports

Anabolic steroid use by elite athletes raises questions that diverge from controversies about drugs like marijuana. Unlike almost all other illegal drugs, steroids are not taken for their effects on the mind. Instead, people use them to build muscle and increase strength. For this reason, the use of anabolic steroids in America does not have the same negative connotations and social stereotypes as the use of other illegal drugs. Steroid users are often the most dedicated athletes in sports. They share many of the dominant values of American society such as intense competition, achievement orientation, and an obsession with fame and money.

The use of anabolic steroids in sports has turned into a public issue. In many cases, fans are far more offended than athletes. Many spectators argue that the use of performance-enhancing drugs gives some athletes an "unfair advantage." They believe that the use of performance-enhancing drugs somehow corrupts the intended purpose of sports or makes a sport easier than it had been in times gone by.

Participation in modern sports develops character and teaches participants to do their best and learn from their experiences. However, elite sports in the twenty-first century are also a massive billion-dollar business. Patriotism, personal rivalry, drug abuse, greed, commercial interests, television, and the erosion of traditional values all influence the modern athletic experience. In elite sports, as in most intensely competitive situations, participants do not expect good sportsmanship but only that their opponents will pursue their self-interest. Victory is the purpose of elite athletics and can be achieved by only one of the competitors or teams. The English writer George Orwell noted that "serious sport has nothing to do with fair play. It is bound up with hatred, jealousy, boastfulness, disregard of all the rules, and sadistic pleasure in witnessing violence, in other words, it is war minus the shooting." In this environment, cheating is a relative term and the use of steroids to triumph is an entirely rational decision.

Many professional athletes see steroids as little more than a tool to help them do their job in the same way that an office worker views his computer. Once their playing days are over, almost all the athletes stop using steroids. For example, California Governor Arnold Schwarzenegger originally became famous by turning his success in bodybuilding into a career in show business and then politics. Schwarzenegger has never denied that he used steroids. As recently as 1996, he said, "I used steroids. It was a risky thing to do, but I have no regrets. It was what I had to do to compete. The danger with steroids is overuse. I only did it before a difficult competition for two months, but not for a period of time that could harm me. And then afterward, it was over. I would stop. I have no health problems, no kidney damage, or anything like that from using them." Only after becoming governor of California did Schwarzenegger's statements become increasingly "anti-steroid." Should the governor of California be considered a "loser" or a "drug cheat" based on his steroid use?

There is rarely a day when anabolic steroids issues are not in the news. Steroids are used in almost every sport. There is a great deal of debate about what the International Olympic Committee (IOC), the major professional sports leagues, and the National

California governor and one-time bodybuilder Arnold Schwarzenegger openly admits to having used steroids "back in the day." Here he congratulates Dexter Jackson for his win in the 2006 Arnold Classic.

Collegiate Athletic Association (NCAA) should do regarding testing for anabolic steroids and enforcement of a steroid ban.

This book explores some of the moral, ethical, and social questions surrounding the use of anabolic steroids in society in general and sports in particular. A controversy is a dispute in which there is strong disagreement, debate, or argument on a matter of opinion. The role of anabolic steroids in society and in sports has been controversial for the last thirty years. On this question, reasonable people of good will can disagree.

2 What Are Anabolic Steroids?

Testosterone

Steroids are synthetic substances related to naturally produced sex hormones such as testosterone. Testosterone is produced in both the male testes and female ovaries. However, testosterone is present in males in much higher levels than in females.

The effects of steroids imitate most of the effects of testosterone. Two of the main effects of testosterone are called *androgenic* and *anabolic*. Androgenic changes involve secondary sexual characteristics in males, such as the growth of facial hair and the deepening of the voice. Anabolic changes include the development of many body tissues such as muscles and skeletal tissue.

Testosterone, as well as other hormones, is responsible for the "masculinizing" effects of male puberty. When males reach the end of puberty, the amount of testosterone rises and stays at a high level for about six months before returning to normal. This surge in testosterone completes the sexual maturation of males. During this time, the growth plates in the long bones of the arms and the legs close, facial hair begins to grow, and the male sex organs grow in size.

At one time, scientists believed they could create steroids that separated the androgenic and anabolic functions. Then it would be possible to build up muscle tissue without causing side effects. However, it now seems that both the anabolic and androgenic effects are caused by the same chemical action on different tissue types.

As of 2009, no one has been able to separate the two properties completely. Therefore, the proper term for these human-made compounds is anabolic-androgenic steroids. However, most people refer to them as anabolic steroids.

The Discovery of Testosterone

Castration is the removal of the testicles of any male animal. People have practiced the castration of animals at least since 4000 BCE to domesticate animals for work and meat production. People quickly noticed that the castration of the male results both in the loss of fertility and secondary sex characteristics. This indicated to ancient people that the testes were somehow involved in the development of "maleness."

Until the mid–1800s, however, most scientists believed the changes after castration occurred through the working of the nervous system. Arnold Berthold (1803–1861) of Gottingen, Germany, the curator of a local zoo, showed otherwise. Berthold conducted some of the earliest experiments to investigate the function of the testes. He performed tests on roosters in 1849 and discovered that the rooster's comb was an androgen-dependent feature. When Berthold castrated some roosters, he observed that their combs wasted away, aggressive male behavior disappeared, and the roosters lost interest in the hens. Berthold also found that he could reverse these castration-induced changes. When he transplanted testes into castrated roosters, the comb grew back and the rooster's behavior changed once again.

Berthold concluded that since the transplanted testes no longer had their nerve connections, the changes did not work through the nervous system. Instead, testes must secrete something into the bloodstream that traveled to the target tissues to cause and maintain these changes. Berthold claimed, "The testes act upon the blood, and the blood acts upon the whole organism."

A generation later, Charles-Édouard Brown-Séquard (1817–1894) conducted new experiments. He injected extracts from animal testes into himself as well as into a range of animals. Brown-Séquard popularized Berthold's idea of substances secreted into the bloodstream and affecting distant organs. These substances are now known as hormones.

On June 1, 1889, Brown-Séquard caused a sensation. He presented a report that claimed he had reversed his own decline into old age by injecting himself with a fluid prepared from the testicles of guinea pigs and dogs. He claimed this "rejuvenating" liquid helped prolong human life. Although this "discovery" turned out to be false, Brown-Séquard's extravagant claims and self-experimentation stimulated the study of the function of the testes and the male reproductive tract.

Medical Uses of Testosterone Derivatives

In the mid–1930s, two separate research teams isolated a substance known as androsterone and converted it to testosterone. Rival chemical companies now tried to discover a more effective version of testosterone. The Croatian scientist Leopold Ruzicka and the German Nazi scientist Adolf Butenandt shared the Nobel Prize for chemistry in 1939 for their work in creating artificial testosterone.

Doctors originally used testosterone derivatives to treat men and women with abnormal hormone production. These treatments worked almost the same as the ancient transplantation of testicular tissue. The first documented case of the use of testosterone to treat a patient was by J. B. Hamilton in 1937. He used testosterone successfully to cure a patient suffering from sexual underdevelopment.

Since the 1950s, research groups have made changes to the basic structure of testosterone and produced a wide range of closely related substances now sold as anabolic steroids. As of 2009, scientists have developed more than one hundred different types of steroids.

Many doctors hoped that testosterone derivatives were a wonder drug. In the late 1930s and the 1940s, doctors used testosterone-based steroids to treat a wide variety of illnesses ranging from heart disease and breast tumors to depression. Many of these uses are no longer medically accepted. However, anabolic steroids have been shown to enhance the quality of life of patients with a number of disabling conditions related to aging. The American Medical Association (AMA) now lists several medical uses for anabolic steroids. These include:

1. treating persistent anemia when red blood cells cannot regenerate
2. controlling metastatic breast cancer
3. treating hereditary angioedema, a type of fluid leakage under the surface of the skin
4. replacing testosterone in men who have had the testes removed due to testicular cancer
5. treating female menopausal symptoms
6. assisting protein buildup in people weakened after surgery, long-term confinement, malnutrition, or serious illness
7. treating adolescent males with pituitary malfunction when they reach the appropriate age for puberty
8. assisting plasmin production to help prevent blood clots

Not all steroids are anabolic steroids. Widespread media coverage has led many people to confuse anabolic steroids with corticosteroids. Doctors use corticosteroids, such as hydrocortisone, prednisone, prednisolone, betamethasone, and cortisone, to treat many different conditions. Corticosteroids can be used as a cream, inhaled, injected, or swallowed. They provide relief for inflamed areas of the body and lessen swelling, redness, itching, and allergic reactions to foods such as peanuts or shellfish. They also help stop or prevent unwanted bleeding. Inhaled corticosteroids are used for treating chronic asthma and other lung irritations. Oral and injectable corticosteroids are used to treat immune reactions in the body and autoimmune diseases such as some blood disorders, lupus, nephritis, and hepatitis.

The Anabolic Steroid Control Act of 1990

It is important to remember that anabolic steroids have a recognized medical purpose and are not illegal. In the United States, doctors can prescribe steroids for so-called "legitimate medical reasons." Doctors wrote an estimated two million prescriptions for testosterone in 2002. However, in 1990, the U.S. Congress made anabolic steroids a controlled substance and doctors could no longer prescribe them for "performance enhancement" or for cosmetic reasons.

The roots of the Anabolic Steroid Control Act date back to the 1980s when U.S. politicians became concerned with the increasing use of steroids in professional, amateur, and even high school sports. The steroid issue achieved national prominence in 1988 when Canadian sprinter Ben Johnson won the one-hundred-meter race at the Summer Olympics in Korea. Johnson was later disqualified and stripped of his medal when he tested positive for steroids.

As a result, the U.S. Congress held hearings from 1988 to 1990 to determine the extent of the steroid problem. Many expert witnesses at the Congressional hearings opposed listing anabolic steroids as controlled substances. These witnesses included the AMA, the Drug Enforcement Administration (DEA), the Food and Drug Administration (FDA), as well as the National Institute on Drug Abuse (NIDA). They maintained that the use of these synthetic hormones does not lead to the physical or psychological dependence that was a requirement for listing a drug under the Controlled Substances Act.

Nevertheless, for political reasons, Congress did add anabolic steroids to Schedule III of the Controlled Substances Act in 1990.

They are in the same legal class as stimulants, codeine derivatives, and central nervous system depressants like barbiturates. Steroids are the only hormones listed in the law. The act defined anabolic steroids as virtually any drug or hormonal substance chemically and pharmacologically related to testosterone that promotes muscle growth. The Anabolic Steroid Control Act of 2004 added prohormones like androstenedione to the list of controlled substances. The 2004 law also removed the phrase that it is a substance that "promotes muscle growth."

The Control Act made it unlawful for any person to possess an anabolic steroid unless it was obtained by a valid prescription from a doctor. This criminalized the nonmedical use of steroids by anyone seeking muscle growth for athletic or cosmetic enhancement. People who are caught illegally possessing anabolic steroids, even for purely personal use, face arrest and prosecution.

Under the law, a conviction for a first offense of simple possession of steroids can be punished by up to one year in jail and/or a minimum fine of $1,000. Distributing anabolic steroids, or possessing them with intent to distribute, is a federal felony punishable by up to five years in prison and/or a $250,000 fine. Penalties are higher for repeat offenders.

Sources of Illegal Steroids

After the Anabolic Steroid Control Act of 1990, most American drug companies stopped manufacturing or marketing steroids in the United States. However, illegal steroids are quite common. They are often purchased from dealers just like any other illegal drug. Illegal steroids are sometimes sold at gyms, sporting competitions, and through the mail. They can also be obtained from pharmacists, veterinarians, and physicians. Black market steroids in America are produced in secret laboratories, smuggled from foreign nations, or illegally diverted from legal sources.

The legal status of anabolic steroids varies from country to

In 2007, the U.S. Drug Enforcement Agency arrested more than 120 people and confiscated more than 11 million units of steroids in the largest sting ever.

country. Anabolic steroids are illegal without a prescription in Argentina, Brazil, and Portugal.

On the other hand, anabolic steroids are easily available without a prescription in some countries such as Mexico and Thailand. About 80 percent of anabolic steroids in the United States comes from Mexico. Many *farmacias* in border towns such as Tijuana sell steroids as an over-the-counter item for the American trade.

In Canada, anabolic steroids are part of the Controlled Drugs and Substances Act and are Schedule IV substances. This means it is illegal to obtain or sell them without a prescription but a person cannot be punished for mere possession of steroids. People who buy or sell anabolic steroids in Canada can be imprisoned up to eighteen months.

In Great Britain, the Misuse of Drugs Act classified anabolic steroids as Class C drugs. This means it is legal to possess steroids in quantities for personal use. However, it is illegal to produce, possess, supply, import, or export steroids without government clearance. Penalties can range from five years' imprisonment to an unlimited fine.

In the 2000s, the worldwide trade in illegal steroids increased significantly despite record steroid seizures by law enforcement agencies. In 2006, Finnish authorities seized 11.8 million steroid tablets. In 2007, the U.S. DEA confiscated 11.4 million units of illegal steroids, the largest American seizure ever. This enormous international investigation involved suppliers in China, Mexico, Canada, Australia, Germany, and Thailand. The DEA made 124 arrests and targeted foreign companies that produced raw materials for producing steroids and human growth hormone. Yet it is not clear whether these successful interdictions affected the market or even the supply of steroids in any meaningful way.

Who Uses Illegal Steroids?

Because most anabolic steroid users in the United States are breaking the law, it is difficult to get accurate data as to who uses them. However, studies have produced some general numbers and concepts. It is estimated that at least a million Americans have used steroids, with percentages highest in the eighteen-to-thirty-four-year-old age bracket. Many Americans use illegal anabolic steroids in order to build muscles, reduce body fat, and improve sports performance. Steroid use is estimated to be very high among competitive bodybuilders and may be widespread in many sports including football, swimming, cycling, wrestling, and baseball.

However, professional and serious amateur athletes actually make up the smallest group of steroid users. They are the best known because the percentage of users within this group is higher than the general population. It is not clear how widespread steroid use is among elite athletes. Severe penalties by sporting bodies discourage athletes from admitting steroid use. If drug testing is accurate, which is unlikely, then the number is somewhere around one percent in the eighteen-to-thirty-four age group.

Numerous studies have shown that Americans who are not involved in any elite sport use anabolic steroids for noncompetitive cosmetic use. This usage is fueled by mass media in the United States, which popularizes large muscles as the standard for male attractiveness. Magazines, advertisements, and music videos all emphasize images of males with "ripped" physiques. Some men who use steroids think their own bodies are small and weak. Boys sometimes see steroids as a quick way to escape the limits of adolescence and move into adulthood.

Some people find steroid use helpful for their careers. Fashion models, film actors, popular culture celebrities, and dancers occasionally take steroids in order to look lean and muscular. Bouncers, police officers, and soldiers might use steroids because additional strength gives them a psychological boost and makes them feel they can perform their job more effectively. Steroid use is by no means limited to athletes.

Female steroid use leads to relatively greater increases in muscle strength and mass than males. Yet steroid use remains higher among males than females. Most Americans view the ideal female body differently than the ideal male body. Some people retain a stigma against muscular or overly competitive women. For many, these traits remain associated with masculinity. However, steroid use seems to be growing most rapidly among young women.

Many nonathletes use steroids to build up their bodies or improve their self-image, among them bouncers such as this man.

Adolescent Steroid Use

Most adolescent anabolic steroid users are not looking to improve their sporting performance. Instead, these teenagers want to "improve" their bodies or their appearance. They might have a negative body image or just have a healthy desire to be stronger. Most of these people are males and they typically use steroids without any medical supervision at all.

In 2007, a government survey of adolescent steroid use concluded that anabolic steroid use by teenagers was down by about half from their peak levels around 2000.

	Boys	Girls
8th graders	1.1%	0.4%
10th graders	1.7%	0.4%
12th graders	2.3%	0.6%

However, the percentage of adolescents who claim to see "great risk" in using steroids once or twice has gradually declined over the last twenty years. In 2007, 57 percent of twelfth graders perceived a "great risk" in occasional steroid use. At the same time, about 90 percent of adolescents say they disapprove of people using steroids even once or twice.

Most high school students have no problem finding steroids if they want to take them. The perceived availability of steroids increases with grade level; by twelfth grade, about 40 percent of adolescents say steroids are "fairly easy" or "very easy" to acquire.

Dosage, Cycling, Stacking, Pyramiding

Anabolic steroids can be used several ways. They are used legally with a prescription for medical conditions. People also use steroids for cosmetic reasons (to look better) and for competitive reasons (to perform better in their chosen sport). Steroids can be taken orally as tablets or capsules, by injections into muscles (the most popular way), or as gels or creams that are rubbed into the skin. People who use steroids take an extremely wide range of dosages. Endurance athletes tend to use low doses. Athletes in sports where bulk is desirable, such as football or weightlifting, use doses as much as one hundred times greater than the doses used to treat medical conditions. Nonathletes might use doses anywhere in between.

Because anabolic steroids enhance performance by enhancing training, elite athletes generally "cycle" steroids. They take steroids for several weeks (the "on cycle") followed by several weeks of nonuse (the "off cycle") to allow the body to recover. The length of these cycles varies a great deal, but most athletes use steroids for six to twelve weeks on and then a similar period off. Power lifters are an exception; they often take the drugs on a relatively continuous basis. However, the use of anabolic steroids in sports is illegal. Therefore, athletes stop using steroids before a competition that might involve a drug test.

People often take anabolic steroids in combination in a practice called *stacking*. Stacking means mixing several different types of steroids at one time. Some steroid users believe stacking is more effective than using only one type of steroid. Users sometimes *pyramid* stacked compounds in cycles of six to twelve weeks, gradually increasing the dose and then slowly decreasing it to zero. Steroid users believe that stacking and pyramiding produce bigger muscles and allow the body to adjust to and recover from high doses of steroids. It is almost impossible to verify or disprove the effectiveness of stacking or pyramiding because steroid strategies vary widely from user to user.

Designer Steroids

Designer steroids are chemical modifications of existing steroid molecules. In this way, chemists can create a new substance with substantial anabolic properties that has not been discovered during previous routine urine testing. Designer steroids are made specifically for athletes. They have no approved medical use and have not been tested or approved by the Food and Drug Administration (FDA).

Norbolethone was a steroid that had been developed in the 1960s but it had never been marketed because of safety concerns. In 1999, the Bay Area Laboratory Co-Operative (BALCO) mixed it with epitestosterone, a masking agent designed to deceive drug testers, and sold it on the black market as "The Cream." Because no one had ever marketed norbolethone, there was no drug test for it. However, it was not technically a designer steroid. Norbolethone was not specifically created to beat anti-doping tests although that became its ultimate use.

On the other hand, tetrahydrogestrinone (THG) was a true designer steroid. It was created solely for use by elite athletes. BALCO made THG by making changes to the chemical structure of a steroid used by cattle farmers to increase animal bulk. The new steroid was extremely effective. For a time, THG was the drug of choice for safe and "invisible" record breaking in athletics. BALCO called it "The Clear." Several famous track stars such as Marion Jones and Dwain Chambers used THG. It was extremely potent and completely undetectable until a track coach submitted a syringe of it to American drug-testing authorities in 2003.

The discovery of a designer steroid such as THG seems to imply there are other designer steroids being used without the possibility of detection. How many are there? No one knows for sure.

Andro and Other Prohormones

Steroid precursors, such as androstenedione (known as andro) and dehydroepiandrosterone (DHEA), are substances that the human body converts into testosterone. Andro is a hormone produced by the adrenal glands, ovaries, and testes. It was first sold in the United States in the mid–1990s.

Andro is not technically a steroid but a steroid precursor (sometimes known as a "prohormone") that helps build muscle.

Creatine

Many athletes take nutritional supplements instead of or in addition to anabolic steroids. Supplements are available over-the-counter at drugstores and health food stores. Americans spent more than $22 billion on nutritional supplements in 2006.

The most popular supplement among athletes is probably creatine monohydrate. Creatine is a naturally occurring chemical produced in the human body from amino acids. It is made mainly in the kidneys and liver and transported in the blood for use by muscles and nerve cells. Creatine helps muscles make and circulate more adenosine triphosphate (ATP), the substance which stores and transports energy in cells.

Creatine is chemically unrelated to anabolic steroids or andro but it is often lumped in with them as a "performance-enhancing substance." Creatine does not manipulate hormone levels but instead allows muscle cells to delay fatigue and recover more quickly. As of 2009, creatine supplements are legal in the United States. It is available in powder, capsule, chew tablet, effervescent tablet, and liquid forms. The compound is considered a dietary supplement and not a drug by the FDA.

Studies have demonstrated that creatine caused modest increases in strength in people with a variety of disorders such as arthritis, congestive heart failure, and muscular dystrophy. It may improve athletic performance during brief, intense activities such as sprinting or weightlifting. In the 1990s, creatine became popular as a "natural" way to enhance athletic performance. In 2003, creatine sales totaled $193 million, or about 10 percent of the sports supplement market. Among sports supplements, only protein powder is more popular.

The use of creatine by healthy people is considered safe if taken at the doses recommended by manufacturers. The effect of long-term creatine use is unknown. The American College of Sports Medicine advises against adolescents taking creatine. In 2000, the National Collegiate Athletic Association (NCAA) banned colleges from distributing creatine to their players. However, the International Society of Sports Nutrition believes that creatine use for serious high school athletes can serve as an alternative to illegal steroids.

The use of creatine is particularly popular among adolescent athletes, who often exceed recommended loading and maintenance doses. A survey of Wisconsin high school athletes published in 2002 found that nearly 17 percent of 4,011 high school athletes, and more than 30 percent of football players, said they had used creatine. Almost one in five said their parents had encouraged them to use creatine, and 26 percent said their coaches had encouraged the supplement's use.

Creatine, andro, and anabolic steroids all increase a naturally occurring substance in the body to promote the building of muscle tissue. Anabolic steroids simply accomplish this end more quickly and dramatically.

However, it is chemically very close to testosterone and is now usually included in lists of steroids. Andro supposedly causes an increase in testosterone levels when ingested. The drug was widely promoted by nutritional supplement companies and bodybuilding magazines for its ability to allow athletes to train harder and recover more quickly.

Andro became a household word in the United States in the summer of 1998. That year, Mark McGwire and Sammy Sosa engaged in an amazing home run contest in which both sluggers shattered the single-season home run record. McGwire finished the season with seventy homers and Sosa had sixty-six. In August, a reporter discovered that McGwire was using andro to build muscles. Andro was not a banned substance in baseball at the time. McGwire specifically said, "Everything I've done is natural. Everybody I know in the game of baseball uses the same stuff I use." However, other sports organizations, including the National Football League, had already banned andro because of its similarity to many steroids.

In 2004, the U.S. Congress added prohormones to the list of controlled substances. This made possession of these substances without a prescription a federal crime. However, andro is still pro-duced in countries such as Mexico, Russia, and Thailand, and is widely available on the U.S. black market. As of 2009, DHEA is the only prohormone still available over-the-counter as a diet supplement.

HGH

Another substance often classified (erroneously) with steroids is human growth hormone, known as HGH. It was developed by bio-technology researchers to treat dwarfism in children, and other serious medical problems. HGH is produced naturally in the body and is essential for growth and development. It helps regulate height, muscle, and organ growth, and plays a role in sexual development.

HGH has been available in a synthetic form since 1985. In the late 1990s, doctors began to tout HGH as a "Fountain of Youth" drug. It has become a $2 billion a year business, involving thousands of people, often promoted with the claim that it has antiaging or athletic-enhancing properties. A number of studies have shown that HGH use does not increase muscle strength in healthy subjects or well-trained athletes. However, many athletes dispute these findings. They claim HGH works like a steroid to boost muscle mass, promote tissue repair, and speed up recovery times between training.

HGH can have serious side effects. Heavy use may change a mature person's body structure and facial characteristics. The most common side effect is acromegaly (the enlargement of hands, feet, and face). High dosage HGH users display swollen heads and protruding brows and jaws. Another possible side effect is gigantism—the overgrowth of the entire body in children or adolescents.

As of 2009, prescribing and distributing HGH for antiaging and bodybuilding is illegal. Yet one of HGH's main attractions for athletes is that, as of 2009, it could be detected only in blood tests, not the standard urine test used for other performance-enhancing drugs.

The Problems of Steroid Research

Much of the controversy surrounding anabolic steroids involves their potential danger to the user. Steroids are drugs. They create multiple actions that affect the human body. All drugs can have adverse side effects, including serious ones that can truly harm the body and mind, and steroids are no exception. But how dangerous are they?

Obviously, a book of this nature cannot definitively make a statement about the possible dangers of the side effects of steroids.

Doctors and scientists have done hundreds, if not thousands, of studies involving steroid usage, yet the effects of steroids remain controversial. Many studies have produced different outcomes, and almost no conclusions can be considered definitive as of 2009. This is mainly because of the difficulty in producing controlled studies of an illegal drug. There are too many variables to sort out; steroid users come from different health backgrounds, take different dosages of different steroids for different lengths of time and in different regimens. This makes it almost impossible to analyze any steroid individually and rules out a definitive cause-and-effect relationship between steroid use and side effects or disease process.

Most conclusions on the dangers of anabolic steroids come from animal studies. Rats subjected to doses approximately equal to illegal steroid use in humans had dramatically reduced life expectancy from a variety of tumors, heart problems, and other medical problems. However, this type of animal data does not always apply to humans. The occurrence of disease in one species does not necessarily mean the same results will occur in another.

The most extensive research on steroid use side effects in humans has been in treating severe illness. Tens of thousands of Americans take anabolic steroids for a variety of medical conditions legally. However, this population is a very different population from illegal steroid users, who are usually "healthy" individuals or well-conditioned athletes. It is therefore difficult to apply these research findings with any degree of certainty.

In addition, steroid use without a prescription is illegal in the United States. It is hard to know how frequently side effects occur because people do not report them. Medical ethics prohibit scientific studies placing human subjects at risk of damaging their health. This has prevented the scientific study of the massive doses of steroids taken by people to obtain an athletic advantage. Therefore, the danger of steroid use is severely contested terrain.

How Dangerous Are Steroids?

At the very least, there are health risks involved in the self-administration of any prescription medicine. People using anabolic steroids without a doctor's advice or monitoring of the correct dose and duration of use risk severe problems. It's also possible that severe side effects may go unnoticed or untreated until it is too late.

As of 2009, the incidence of recorded death or life-threatening diseases associated with anabolic steroid use is relatively low. Most severe problems are anecdotal and have been linked to long-term and high-dose use. It is possible that for most people, the side effects of anabolic steroid use appear to be minimal. Many changes in the body may return to normal after steroid use is stopped. On the other hand, there is enough data to conclude that there is at least an association between steroid use and significant negative side effects.

Anabolic steroids seem to increase the risk of elevated blood pressure, cardiovascular disease, high cholesterol levels, or coronary artery disease. Even if these changes are temporary, steroid users are exposing themselves to the premature development of vascular and coronary heart disease. Some studies imply that steroids can even change the structure of the heart, impairing its contraction and relaxation. Possible effects of these alterations in the heart are hypertension, irregular heartbeat, congestive heart failure, and heart attacks. These changes also occur in non-steroid-using athletes, but anabolic steroid use may accelerate this process. However, all these findings have been disputed.

High doses of oral anabolic steroid compounds may cause liver damage. The liver is the main organ that breaks down steroids in the

Steroid use by teenagers is hotly contested. Here, Don Hooton looks at the photo of his deceased son, Taylor. Taylor is believed to have killed himself because he became depressed after he stopped using steroids.

digestive system. Many studies of steroid users have documented abnormalities in liver function tests. However, the seriousness of these abnormalities and their duration is still disputed.

Less seriously, acne is common among anabolic steroid users, caused by increased testosterone levels. The conversion of testosterone can also accelerate the rate of premature baldness for those who are genetically predisposed.

There are also some gender-specific side effects of anabolic steroids. Males may develop breast tissue (known as gynecomastia), temporary infertility (although sexual drive might actually increase), and testicular atrophy. Steroid use may also be linked with prostate cancer. Female-specific side effects include increases in body hair, deepening of the voice, and enlarged genitals. When taken during pregnancy, anabolic steroids can affect fetal development.

One area where there is almost no debate is the negative effect of anabolic steroids on still-growing adolescent users. For adolescents, steroid use may halt bone growth and result in stunted growth. Other effects include accelerated bone maturation and premature sexual development. These side effects are particularly dangerous because teenagers are more likely than adults to use anabolic steroids in dangerously high dosages and without any medical supervision.

On a comparative scale, however, anabolic steroids are less dangerous than most common drugs. In 2007, a group of scientists attempted to create a new ranking system by assessing twenty different drugs based on their potential for addiction and the harm they do to the individual and to society. The experts rated heroin as the most dangerous drug, followed by cocaine and barbiturates. Anabolic steroids only ranked sixteenth out of twenty, far below alcohol and tobacco.

However, the long-term consequences of steroid use have not been well investigated. It is possible that more severe side effects will occur later in the life of anabolic steroid users.

Are Steroids Addictive?

Anabolic steroids are not physically addictive. Users can stop taking them without physical withdrawal symptoms. (Withdrawal refers to newly experienced physical or psychological feelings of distress that occur when the user stops using a drug.)

However, steroids have the potential to be psychologically addictive. This means that people experience a compulsion to take a drug even though they know there might be adverse consequences that result from drug use. There are not many large-scale long-term studies of the psychiatric effects of steroids. Animal studies have shown that anabolic steroids are reinforcing. For example, animals will self-administer some types of steroids when given the opportunity, just as they do with other addictive drugs. This property is more difficult to demonstrate in humans.

Certainly, some users keep taking steroids in spite of the cost, physical problems, negative effects on social relations, and increased nervousness or irritability. Others experienced typical withdrawal symptoms when they stopped taking steroids, such as depression, major mood swings, fatigue, loss of appetite, and reduced sex drive. These are symptoms of dependence or psychological addiction.

However, not everyone who takes anabolic steroids experiences these symptoms. Tens of thousands of users have quit and experienced no symptoms at all. One expert believes a quarter to a half of those who use steroids solely to improve their body image exhibit signs of psychological dependence. A much smaller group experience symptoms of psychological dependence needing clinical treatment. The exact relationship between the use of anabolic steroids and psychological addiction is not yet clear.

'Roid Rage

Scientists are nearly unanimous that excessive testosterone causes aggression in rats and monkeys, but this association is not clear in humans. Anecdotal evidence seems to indicate that high-dose anabolic steroid users sometimes experience short temper, extreme irritability, and elevated feelings of aggression. These symptoms of heavy steroid use are sometimes called "'roid rage." The media has popularized stories linking steroids with murder, domestic violence, armed robbery, child abuse, and road rage.

However, there is no agreement among doctors or researchers as to whether "'roid rage" actually exists. Some studies report no increase in aggression or hostility with steroid use. Anabolic steroids tend to amplify traits a user already possesses. A steroid user with anger problems is more likely to experience heightened aggression. However, "aggression" is not clearly defined or easily quantified. The fact that a steroid user self-reports that she or he feels more aggressive does not necessarily mean that the person is on the verge of violent behavior.

Clinical and anecdotal reports suggest that anabolic steroids may contribute to psychiatric problems involving increased aggression. However, an extremely small percentage of the estimated one million past or current steroid users in the United States appear to have experienced mental disturbance severe enough to result in clinical treatments. This ambiguity of all the research data on anabolic steroids leads to the controversy over steroid use.

3 The Use of Anabolic Steroids in Sports

"Doping" in Sports

There was never a "Golden Age" of sport when all competitors relied on talent alone. Better training, improved technology, or performance-enhancing substances have been present in sports for hundreds of years. Participants in every sport have tried to gain an edge over their rivals. By definition, sport involves competition and almost every competitor plays to win. As far back as the ancient Greek Olympics, competitors put their faith in eating a variety of things—figs, sesame seeds, wine, meat, mushrooms—to aid performance.

In the late 1800s, athletes used stimulants based on drugs made from South American and African plants. The word "dope" first appeared in an English dictionary in 1889. Dope was an opium-based mixture given to horses so they would run faster and not get hurt. Cyclers, swimmers, and boxers all took dope to enhance their performance. At first, many people viewed the use of drugs in a positive light. In the hundred years before World War I, people embraced the concept of "progress." Scientists, athletes, and much of the public believed that drugs had the potential to improve society by improving the human body.

Stimulants such as strychnine and ephedrine were especially popular in sporting communities. Amphetamines (first created in 1887) and methamphetamine (known as "speed" and first produced in 1919) were widely used. Some nations experimented with the

Hitler's Nazi Party hosted the 1936 Olympics. They took the majority of the medals, and proclaimed their superiority in sports to be just one aspect of the superiority of the "pure" Germanic race that would exist when they eliminated the other, "lesser" races.

use of amphetamines for soldiers as a way to solve the problem of fatigue. As fast as scientists invented new drugs, athletes tried them out. In the early 1900s, scientific research into the human body began to show that interval training, resistance training, and varying the level of exercise intensity could improve athletic performance. Participants and spectators saw the link between science knowledge and success in sports.

The desirability of using drugs in sports became more important in the 1920s and 1930s. Modern athletics became increasingly affected by money and politics. As leisure time in modern societies increased, winning offered fame and financial wealth to successful competitors. The monetary rewards of a successful sporting career became equal to one in politics, the military, or even business. Figures like Babe Ruth (baseball), Red Grange (football), Bill Tilden (tennis), and Jack Dempsey (boxing) became mythic American celebrities. In 1936, Adolf Hitler made a great propaganda show of hosting the Summer Olympics in Berlin. Despite the four individual gold medals by African American Jesse Owens, Germany topped the medal table. Nazi propagandists used the results of the Olympics to reinforce their claim to racial superiority. Sports were no longer peripheral activities of little importance.

After World War II, many athletes were entangled in the cold war between the United States and the Soviet Union. Both sides tried to prove the superiority of their political and economic systems in any way possible. Sports became a propaganda tool and athletic success was closely tied to nationalism and patriotism. Countries now tried to "win" the Olympics, and medal counts by nation became very important. Some events, such as the Hungarian defeat of the Soviet water polo team (1956), or the U.S. gold medal in ice hockey (1980), took on huge symbolic significance. By the 1970s, elite sports had become deadly serious, filled with athletes obsessed with winning. The media, advertisers, spectators, and sports governing bodies all wanted to witness great events with heroic athletes breaking world records. In this atmosphere, athletes, coaches, and government officials all saw the value of anabolic steroids.

Anabolic Steroids Enter Sports

Steroids entered the American competitive world when bodybuilders in California discovered the drug after World War II. Steroids helped muscle growth and limited the breakdown of protein in muscle cells. Bodybuilders quickly realized steroids could increase the muscle gain resulting from strenuous exercise and maximize the effect of a high protein diet.

In 1954, American physician John Ziegler attended the world weightlifting championships in Vienna, Austria. At this competition, a Russian doctor told him how hormonal treatments had greatly enhanced the performance of Soviet athletes. Ziegler himself witnessed athletes taking testosterone. Ziegler was not filled with moral outrage. He simply decided that the American weightlifters also needed to use drugs in order to compete effectively. When Ziegler returned to the United States, he received funding from the drug company Ciba and helped synthesize the first so-called anabolic steroid—Dianabol, also known as methandrostenolone. Ciba released it in the United States in 1958.

Anabolic steroids quickly became an essential part of the bodybuilding, weightlifting, and cycling subcultures. News of the effectiveness of these new drugs spread by word of mouth to competitors in other strength-intensive sports. Almost all the best American throwers in field sports of that era tried anabolic steroids, including Randy Matson (1968 Olympic champion and world record holder in the shot put), Dallas Long (1964 Olympic shot put champion), Harold Connolly (1956 Olympic champion in the hammer throw), and Russ Hodge (world record holder in the decathlon). None of these athletes received major criticism because in the 1960s, anabolic steroid use was not banned at the Olympics. Athletes and coaches did not question the morality of taking anabolic steroids; the only debate was over which drugs were more effective.

In the 1970s, the use of steroids spread from strength-dependent sports such as weightlifting and field events into other sports such as hockey, swimming, baseball, and track. Athletes realized that steroids reduced the soreness that normally results from strenuous exercise. Steroids allowed the user to train for longer periods at a more intensive level without injury. For many elite athletes, recovery time was the key to their training. The sooner their bodies could recover from an intense workout or painful game, the sooner they could return to the practice field or weight room. This was one of the greatest benefits of steroids, equally important to explosive muscle growth.

The Scientific Community Decides Steroids Work

In the 1970s, the medical and sporting establishments could not decide whether anabolic steroids aided athletic performance and, if so, what to do about them. In 1975, the British Association of Sport and Medicine's official policy stated that "no known chemical agent is capable of producing both safely and effectively an improvement in performance in a healthy human subject." In 1977, the American College of Sports Medicine (ACSM) wrote in their annual report that there was no conclusive evidence that steroids improved athletic performance. One ACSM member suggested that steroids were merely placebos.

Athletes knew better. By the late 1970s, they were convinced of the advantages of anabolic steroids. This caused a major gap in credibility between athletes and the scientific community. From 1950 to 1980, athletes who used anabolic steroids were astounded that sporting bodies could deny the anecdotal and even scientific evidence of the positive effect on their performance.

In the 1980s, sporting authorities and scientists finally accepted that anabolic steroids could produce an improvement in athletic performance. They identified three conditions that had to be fulfilled for steroids to be effective:

1. The athlete must have been undergoing an intensive weightlifting program before starting on steroids.
2. The athlete must continue this intensive training program throughout the course of steroid use.
3. The athlete must eat a high protein diet.

In other words, a couch potato cannot take anabolic steroids and turn into an elite athlete. Steroids help athletes train harder and recover more quickly from breakdown but there are limits to what steroids can do. Athletes who want results need to work out. Nor can anabolic steroid drugs produce a skill such as balance or hand-eye coordination. However, for men or women with an athletic gift and self-discipline, anabolic steroids could make them bigger and stronger.

The medical and sporting establishments now had a problem. They had to find some way of keeping athletes from using drugs that scientific research had proven to enhance performance. There was already a significant lack of trust between the sports medicine and athletic communities. Many athletes distrusted doctors' claims that steroids were potentially dangerous. Many used extremely high dosages for the sake of their career.

Ben Johnson at the 1988 Summer Olympics

For years, athletes and spectators had suspected Eastern European athletes used anabolic steroids. But the 1988 Summer Olympics marked a major turning point in the public's view of sport. For the first time, spectators had to face the fact that the world's greatest athletes often used drugs and chemicals to enhance their performances.

Ben Johnson looks rather irritated in this photo taken at the 1988 Seoul Olympic Games. When he was stripped of his medal because of steroid use, many fans were disgusted.

The scandal centered around Ben Johnson, a Canadian sprinter who had set a one-hundred-meter world record (9.83 seconds) at the 1987 World Championships in Rome. Johnson became a famous marketing celebrity, earning about $480,000 a month in endorsements. The Associated Press named Johnson "Athlete of the Year" for 1987.

In the 1988 Olympics, Johnson broke the world record (9.79 seconds) again only to have his record erased three days later when he tested positive for stanozolol, a well-known bodybuilder's steroid. He later admitted that he had also used steroids when he ran his 1987 world record, which caused the International Association of Athletics Federations (IAAF) to rescind that record as well. Johnson's fall represented the biggest drug scandal in Olympic history.

Johnson's positive test dramatically increased the level of national and international attention focused on anabolic steroid use. A well-publicized study in the 1988 *Journal of the American Medical Association* suggested that as many as half a million American adolescents might be using steroids. This was one of the factors that led the U.S. Congress to pass the Steroid Control Act in 1990.

However, the use of anabolic steroids continued to grow with the financial rewards of a sporting career. Steroids soon spread to rugby, gymnastics, swimming, lacrosse, volleyball, wrestling, boxing, and soccer. It would take several books to detail all the athletes and sports caught up in controversies over anabolic steroid use. What follows is a brief summary of steroid controversies in several major American and international sports.

Cycling

The sport of cycling has a long history of tacit acceptance of drug use. In 1930, the rule book for the Tour de France even reminded riders that drugs would not be provided by the organizers. Until the 1960s, most people in cycling believed there was nothing wrong with the sensible use of stimulants such as amphetamines. This position changed when the Danish cyclist Knud Jensen died at the 1960 Rome Olympics after taking amphetamines. His death was a major factor in motivating the International Olympic Committee (IOC) to begin testing for performance-enhancing drugs at the Olympics.

In the 1970s, cyclists moved away from amphetamines and switched to steroids as the drug of choice. Professional cycling is a difficult endurance sport; cyclists might ride 20,000 miles a year. Jean-Luc Vandenbroucke, a Belgian rider, gave a spirited defense of steroid use. "In the Tour de France, I took steroids," he said. "If I hadn't, I would have had to give up. What do you think? I'm on the bike all year from February onwards, I have to do well in the classics in all the little races, and also in the Tour de France....You can't call that medically harmful, not if it's done under a doctor's control and within reason."

Despite drug testing, major doping scandals continue to rock the cycling world. The most widely abused performance-enhancing drug in cycling is erythropoietin (EPO), a naturally occurring hormone that is not an anabolic steroid. Cyclists inject EPO because it increases the production of red blood cells and allows the blood to carry more oxygen to the muscles.

However, anabolic steroids are still used. In 1998, customs agents stopped Willy Voet, an assistant for the Festina cycling team, at a routine border search. They found a treasure trove of drugs in his car, including steroids, amphetamines, EPO, and masking agents. The Festina scandal rocked the cycling world. An investigation led to the suspension, arrest, and prosecution of a number of riders and team staff members.

The most controversial anabolic steroid case in cycling was probably that of Floyd Landis. Landis, an American cyclist, was stripped of his overall victory in the 2006 Tour de France after a positive test result for anabolic steroids in two urine samples after stage seventeen. Landis vehemently insisted he was not guilty of

"Everyone is entitled to their own opinion, but not their own facts."

The Honorable Daniel Patrick M...

Floyd Landis was convicted of steroid use despite his continued denials. Clearly, many people did not believe him.

using banned steroids, and a drawn-out hearing and appeal follow-ed. Nonetheless, Landis received a two-year ban from professional racing following an arbitration panel's ruling in 2007.

Landis's fate did not seem to solve the problem of drugs in cycling. The 2007 Tour de France was wracked by a series of scandals, accusations, and gossip related to doping. By the end of the tour, several cyclists were dismissed or "retired" for testing positive for drugs or missing drug tests.

Steroids in Baseball

In the United States, the biggest anabolic-steroid scandals have involved baseball players. In the 1990s, the use of steroids coincided with a huge increase in the number of home runs. Although there are many possible reasons for the explosion of home runs, many observers claim steroids have helped build the greatest extended era of slugging that baseball has ever seen. Before 1998, no one ever hit more than sixty-one home runs in a season. From 1998 to 2001, it happened six times. The changes in the game are also evident in the increasingly hulking physiques of the players. The average weight of an All-Star in 1991 was 199 pounds. Ten years later, it was 211.

Several of baseball's biggest sluggers have been implicated in the use of anabolic steroids. In 2005, slugger Jose Canseco admitted to using steroids for years and identified several former teammates, including stars Mark McGwire, Jason Giambi, and Rafael Palmeiro, as fellow steroid users. Most of the players he named denied using steroids but later turned out to be lying.

Ken Caminiti was a solid third baseman of medium build and strong skills who used steroids to turn himself into a muscle-bound slugger when he joined the San Diego Padres in 1995. In 1996, he astounded everyone by hitting forty home runs, fourteen more than he had ever hit in his life. In 2002, Caminiti admitted that he won the 1996 National League Most Valuable Player award while on steroids he purchased from a pharmacy in Tijuana, Mexico.

In 1998, baseball fans and the media were captivated by Mark McGwire's seventy home runs and his duel for the record with Sammy Sosa, who hit sixty-six that year. McGwire has never admitted to or been convicted of any steroid use but most of his statements have now been questioned. McGwire refused to answer questions under oath when he appeared before the U.S. Congress in 2005. Although no action was taken against McGwire, his refusal to talk about steroids cost him public affection and support.

In 2003, Alex Rodriguez won the American League home run title and the Most Valuable Player award as a shortstop for the Texas Rangers. In 2009, Rodriguez's name was leaked as one of the names on the list of 104 players who tested positive for performance-enhancing drugs in 2003 testing. Rodriguez, baseball's highest-paid player as a New York Yankees superstar, admitted that he had taken steroids while playing for the Texas Rangers from 2001 through 2003. Rodriguez was traded from Texas to the Yankees in 2004, three years into a record ten-year contract worth $252 million. "I had just signed this enormous contract," Rodriguez said. "I felt like I needed something, a push, without over-investigating what I was taking, to get me to the next level."

Until 2002, Major League Baseball (MLB) had no steroid policy or testing program at all for major leaguers. As recently as 2004, there was no suspension for a first offense with steroid use. However, negative publicity forced the baseball world to put together a tougher policy. The catalyst was the 409-page "Mitchell Report," the result of a twenty-month investigation (concluding in 2007) into the use of steroids in baseball. The investigation, headed by former U.S. Senate Majority Leader George Mitchell, named eighty-nine major-league baseball players linked to steroids or performance-enhancing drugs. The report used informant testimony and more than 115,000 pages of documents to provide a detailed portrait of what Mitchell called "baseball's steroids era." Mitchell concluded that, "For more than a decade there has been widespread illegal use of anabolic steroids and other performance-enhancing substances by players in Major League Baseball, in violation of federal law and baseball policy. . . . Those who have illegally used these substances range from players whose major league careers were brief to potential members of the Baseball Hall of Fame."

One of the players tied to performance-enhancing drugs in the Mitchell Report was Roger Clemens, the greatest pitcher of his time.

Anabolic steroids help pitchers throw the ball harder, recover faster between games, and maintain strength throughout the season. In the Mitchell Report, former Yankee trainer Brian McNamee stated that during three seasons, he injected Clemens with stanozolol. In 2008, Clemens testified before Congress that he had never used steroids. As of 2009, the truth of the matter is still unresolved.

American Football

Anabolic steroids have been connected with American football since at least the 1960s. However, the issue did not become controversial until the late 1980s. In 1987, the National Football League (NFL) began testing players for steroid use. Two years later, the league started to suspend players for drug use. The NFL's banned substance policy is the longest running in American professional sports.

When the NFL began testing players for anabolic steroids, 30 percent tested positive. A report in 1985 suggested that 95 percent of football players had tried steroids at some time and 75 percent were regular users. Since the NFL began random, year-round tests, more than one hundred NFL players have tested positive for banned substances. The NFL administers about ten thousand tests annually to about 1,800 players. Each player is tested at least once, and seven or eight players from each team are tested at random each week during the season. A player can be tested up to six times in the off-season, although this is quite rare.

Probably the highest profile NFL steroids case involved Shawne Merriman, the 2005 American Football Conference (AFC) Defensive Rookie of the Year. A random drug test revealed that Merriman, a linebacker for the San Diego Chargers, had nandrolone in his urine. Merriman had previously tested clean on nineteen of twenty random tests for performance-enhancing drugs since he entered the league. The NFL suspended Merriman for four games in 2006 even though he insisted the steroids came from a tainted nutritional supplement.

Barry Bonds

When Barry Bonds played for the Pittsburgh Pirates in 1986, he was a slim, 185-pound leadoff hitter. In 1993, he joined the San Francisco Giants and seemed to alter both his size and his game. Bonds grew into a 230-pound force who became the greatest home run hitter of all time. He won a record-setting seven MVP awards, including four in a row. He made the All-Star team fourteen times and holds (as of 2009) the home run record with 762. He also holds the single-season record for home runs (seventy-three), set in 2001.

In 2003, Bonds was linked to the steroids scandal involving his trainer, Greg Anderson, of the Bay Area Laboratory Co-Operative (BALCO). A federal grand jury indicted Anderson for supplying steroids to athletes, including several baseball players. Bonds's connections to BALCO have been a source of controversy for many years. Many people believe that Bonds had used steroids and HGH (before 2003) when there was no mandatory drug testing in baseball.

In 2005, the defendants in the BALCO steroids scandal trial struck deals with federal prosecutors that did not require them to reveal the names of athletes who may have used banned drugs. They all received less than six months of jail time. Anderson, however, served a year in jail for his refusal to testify before a grand jury in 2006 about Bonds's steroid use.

Bonds denied steroid use several times. He insisted his changed body and increased power resulted from intense training, diet, and legitimate supplements. Bonds testified to a grand jury that he used various products supplied by his trainer, including steroids known as "The Cream" and "The Clear." However, he claimed that he did not know what these products contained when he took them. In 2007, Bonds was indicted on four counts of perjury and one count of obstruction of justice regarding his alleged use of steroids. As of 2009, the truth of Bond's involvement with steroids was still unresolved.

The use of anabolic steroids has permeated other levels of American football. The National Collegiate Athletic Association (NCAA) claims that about one percent of all NCAA football players fail drug tests taken at bowl games, and overall, 3 percent have admitted to using steroids. Steroid use at the high school football level doubled from 1991 to 2003. A survey showed that about 6 percent of high school players out of a survey size of 15,000 admitted to using some type of anabolic steroid or performance-enhancing drug at one point in their playing time. Less than 10 percent of high schools have any form of drug-testing program for their football teams.

The staggering size of modern-day football players seems to imply that anabolic steroid use is more widespread than testing data reveals. In 1991, there were eighty-three NFL players weighing at least three hundred pounds; in 2001, there were 290. This trend is found in colleges as well. At the University of Colorado, the average weight of offensive linemen was 189 pounds in 1950, 246 in 1980, and 307 in 2000. However, coaches insist that this has been accomplished through diet, the use of legal nutritional supplements, year-round strength training, and plain hard work.

Weightlifting and Bodybuilding

Weightlifting has the dubious distinction of being the most drug-ridden of Olympic sports. That is not surprising considering that performance-enhancing drugs can make a huge difference in lifting heavy barbells. Technical skill is involved but raw muscle power is essential.

The list of anabolic steroids scandals in weightlifting would make a book in itself. Scandal effects go beyond the accused individuals because they cast suspicion over the entire sport. In the 1988 Olympics in Korea, Bulgaria and Hungary withdrew their weightlifting teams after some of their lifters were expelled from the games following positive drug tests. The negative publicity was

Steroid use has spread to all fields of athletic endeavor, from female runners and bodybuilders to baseball and football megastars.

so bad that the IOC considered completely removing weightlifting as an Olympic sport.

However, recent Olympics have not been noticeably freer of anabolic steroids. In the 2008 Beijing Summer Olympics, Bulgaria was forced to withdraw its entire weightlifting team after eleven athletes tested positive for steroids. At the same Olympics, Greece only sent four competitors after eleven Greek weightlifters were suspended for doping. Both nations were weightlifting powers with previous offenses. Bulgaria was stunned by a doping scandal at the 2000 Olympics when three athletes returned their medals after positive drug tests. In the 2004 Olympics, a Greek weightlifter was stripped of his medal for taking a banned substance. The latest scandals have again triggered calls for weightlifting to be dropped from future Olympics.

Bodybuilding lacks the high profile of weightlifting because it is not an Olympic sport. However, several iconic bodybuilders, such as Arnold Schwarzenegger and Sergio Oliva, have admitted long-term anabolic steroid use before the drug was banned in 1990. Anecdotal evidence implies that many bodybuilders continue to use anabolic steroids for muscle mass gain.

Basketball and Hockey

As of 2009, neither the National Basketball Association (NBA) nor the National Hockey League (NHL) required every player to be tested annually for anabolic steroids. However, both professional leagues toughened their policies after 2005. The NBA policy, in effect until 2011, permits players to be randomly tested no more than four times each season. The NBA suspends players ten games for a first steroids offense, twenty-five games for a second offense, and a year for a third offense. A fourth positive test results in a lifetime ban.

Before 2005, the NHL had almost no drug policy and did not randomly test for banned substances. Then the league began a new anti-doping policy as part of the collective bargaining agreement between the players' union and team owners. This agreement will last through the 2011 season. The new policy stated that every NHL player would be subject to up to two "no-notice" random tests every year, with at least one test conducted on a team-wide basis. Penalties get more severe with each successive failed test: twenty games, sixty games, and a lifetime suspension.

Like elite athletes in most sports, professional basketball and hockey players have been growing bigger and stronger in the last couple of decades. However, the NHL and the NBA both insist that players' use of anabolic steroids is extremely rare. For example, as of 2009, only one player had been suspended for violating the NHL's steroid policy. As always, negative drug-testing results do not necessarily mean that players are not taking steroids.

Hypocrisy by Coaches, Doctors, and Officials

The natural inclination of fans, politicians, the media, and sports federations is to blame the players for the use of anabolic steroids in sports. They all tar the players as drug cheats and corrupt losers who are looking to take advantage of society. However, the pervasive use of steroids could not exist without the complicity of many coaches, doctors, trainers, and sports officials.

In some cases, anabolic steroids have been justified in the name of national pride. In the years of the cold war (from 1945 to 1990 between the United States and the Soviet Union), some doctors in the United States saw it as their patriotic duty to supply steroids to athletes. In those years, large percentages of American Olympic athletes took steroids while officials looked the other way. Sometimes they even took an active role in suppressing the results of drug tests. One doctor for the United States Olympic Committee (USOC) reported that drug-testers used "the sink method" to check for steroids in the 1980s. They collected urine from American medal winners, poured the urine down the sink, and reported that none of the winners tested positive for performance-enhancing drugs. The drug testing was simply designed to convince the American public, media, and wealthy sponsors that there was no drug problem in Olympic sports. The ultimate goal was to keep the American Olympic image clean so everyone connected with it could make money and be happy.

Sometimes, steroid use has gone beyond the informal collusion of elite athletes, coaches, physicians, and sports scientists. Some countries actually created doping programs sponsored and promoted by a national government and sports federation officials. The most famous case is that of East Germany, a power in international sports from 1965 to 1990. Its athletes established numerous world records while using major doses of anabolic steroids and other illegal substances. More than ten thousand unsuspecting young athletes, some only twelve years old, were given massive doses of anabolic steroids. Accusations of similar national doping programs have been made against other nations, most recently China.

In the United States, the Mitchell Report criticized the commissioner's office and the players' union for knowingly tolerating performance-enhancing drugs. It cited many instances where club officials knew about steroid use among players and did not report it. Both the players and the owners have found it tremendously convenient to look the other way. Both sides know that despite some fans' complaints, the "Year of the Home Run" in 1998 was a tremendous success that undid much of the fan anger and economic damage caused by baseball's 1994 to 1995 work stoppage.

Sports are big business in modern societies. The IOC, NCAA, NFL, NBA, and MLB are all billion-dollar businesses. These organizations downplay the role of drugs in sports and occasionally withhold drug-testing information. They do not want to jeopardize the billions of dollars paid by corporate sponsors and television networks for what they present to the world as a clean and wholesome event. Many people depend on athletes and the sports industry for their employment. For coaches, winning enables them to keep their jobs, many of which pay quite well. Coaches demand bigger, stronger, and faster performances from their athletes. They often ignore how these results are achieved.

For example, one NFL Hall of Famer related the following scenario: "Teams draft a kid who looks like he can be a player. But when they get the player at minicamp, they see that he's smaller and not as strong as they thought. They tell him that he's got to be bigger and stronger before he reports to training camp, and he's got eight weeks to do it. There's only so many steak, potatoes and milk shakes you can eat in eight weeks. If the player is up against a time frame, he'll do what he has to do to get the results."

Charles Francis, Ben Johnson's coach, offered few regrets for his role in the steroids scandal. Francis freely admitted that his athletes were taking anabolic steroids. He argued that success in international track and field depends on chemical assistance and that the health hazards of steroids are exaggerated. Johnson said, "If mature and informed elite athletes conclude that they must take steroids to survive in their sport, and can do so without jeopardizing their health, they should be able to make that choice freely." It is this contention that is at the heart of the controversy over steroids.

4 Nonathletic Issues: Paternalism and Drug Testing

The Argument from Harm

The controversy over anabolic steroids is often seen as a problem of athletics. However, the majority of steroid users are not athletes. For them, the controversy over steroids does not involve ethics and cheating. Instead, it hinges on acceptable governmental limits and the accuracy of drug testing.

The most basic argument against anabolic steroid use has nothing to do with sports. Instead, it rests on protecting the physical well-being of individual Americans. Steroids are a Class III drug because users may suffer short- or long-term physical or psychological harm because of their use. Anabolic steroids have been accused of causing harm to the people who take them, other people, the nature of sport, the country, and society in general.

The position that banning steroids is a way of preventing people from hurting themselves is called an "argument from harm." This argument is also the basis for banning other drugs, such as marijuana, cocaine, and heroin. It is important to note that this claim needs to be applied independently to each particular substance in order to carry any weight. It is perfectly logical to support the government's right to outlaw cocaine and yet oppose a ban on anabolic steroids.

Opponents of steroid use claim the drugs are associated with strokes, heart ailments, liver disease, and 'roid rage. Steroid users claim that side effects usually stop when a person stops taking the drug, and that steroid use over a short time span carries little risk. The medical evidence for doctor-supervised steroid use is mixed. Much of the "evidence from harm" is anecdotal and comes from ath-letes using very high doses in uncontrolled conditions.

In general, it seems reasonable to say that anabolic steroids, like all drugs, have side effects. The dangers of serious problems increase with higher doses or long-term use. Of course, the qualifier must be added that the "perceived safety" of steroids depends entirely on the current state of scientific knowledge. Several "safe" drugs have been introduced that turned out to be absolute disasters after some years of use.

However, even assuming that anabolic steroids are dangerous, it does not necessarily follow that there should be laws prosecuting mature adults who take steroids. Supporters of steroid use raise the objection that by regulating steroids, society (and the government) denies men and women their fundamental right to choose. They argue that if some Americans believe steroids improve their looks or athletic performance, they should be free to choose them. If there are any risks, then people can be warned and make an informed choice.

What could possibly be wrong with a policy that saves people from death or illness? Yet Americans do not usually support governmental intrusion into the lives of competent adults based on the idea of protecting them from all possible harm. The vast majority of Americans use at least some of the following: tranquilizers, pain controllers, mood controllers, antidepressants, decongestants, diet pills, birth control pills, caffeine, nicotine, sleep aids, and alcohol. Many of these have the potential to do considerable harm to the individual. Some of these drugs are regulated but some are not. Cigarettes are legal (although not for adolescents), while possession of drugs like marijuana and cocaine is a criminal offense. The argument from harm is more complex than it first appears.

Paternalism and Its Opponents

A *libertarian* believes that the government should not intervene in matters of economics or personal behavior where no one's rights are being threatened or violated. Extreme libertarians consider almost any form of governmental intervention to be unacceptable. However, most Americans accept the notion that there are some acceptable forms of governmental action. The law prohibits driving without a seat belt, locating a factory in a residential neighborhood, or paying workers five cents an hour. In these cases, the government acts like a parent and deprives individuals of freedom and responsibility in the name of ethics, economics, or the greater good. The desire to act on behalf of others or to protect others from the effects of their own actions is known as *paternalism.*

The American government is said to represent the will of the people of the United States. Paternalists believe that Congress, acting for the people, should restrict individuals from doing things shown to be harmful in the past or not useful to a person's individual development. Opponents of anabolic steroid use claim the ban on steroids is an acceptable form of paternalism comparable to laws against jaywalking, heroin use, and polygamy.

John Stuart Mill, a nineteenth-century British philosopher, stated the classic opposition to paternalism. Mill believed each individual has the right to act as he wants so long as those actions do not harm others. If the action only directly affects the person undertaking the action (a "self-regarding" action), then society has no right to intervene, even if it feels the actor is harming himself. Mill wrote, "Mankind are greater gainers by suffering each other to live as seems good to themselves, than by compelling each to live as seems good to the rest."

Nineteenth-century philosopher John Stuart Mill, a libertarian, believed that people had the right to behave as they pleased as long as they did not harm others. Some, of course, would say that steroid use harms the common good.

Mill believed the potential for harm to others is not sufficient reason for social regulation. Some of history's greatest violations of freedom of speech and conscience have occurred when society has criminalized self-regarding actions. Mill claimed that the individual is the "final judge" of personal matters because "he is the person most interested in his own well being."

Certainly, many things are dangerous, although the degree of danger varies from case to case. The use of steroids may have harmful effects on the user. However, steroid users would argue that a steroids ban is an unneeded limitation on individual freedom and personal liberties. At the same time, the law increases governmental power unnecessarily. Governmental intrusion into people's lives risks the creation of a dictatorship; this would be a far greater evil than the possible injury of activities that individuals choose of their own free will.

In the realm of sports, the argument that steroid laws protect athletes from harm is particularly inconsistent. Many sporting activities contain health risks by definition. The law does not prevent people from skiing, scuba diving, mountain climbing, or hang gliding, which are all extremely dangerous activities sometimes involving fatalities. Steroids may be dangerous, but more participants die or are seriously injured from sports such as boxing, football, and auto racing.

However, it might be argued that boxing risks are inherent in that activity, while sprinting risks should not include anabolic steroid use. Some sports contain "necessary risks" that cannot be removed without preventing or significantly changing the nature of the sport. Opponents of steroids argue that steroid use is an "unnecessary risk" not related to the definition of a particular sport.

Informed Consent vs. Paternalism

Perhaps setting up a choice between legal and illegal steroids oversimplifies a complex question. In law, the concept of *informed consent* describes a case where a person must be told the nature and risks of a medical procedure before a doctor can validly claim exemption from responsibility (and liability) for medical problems. In a hospital, most informed consents are written and signed by the patient or a legal representative. However, in the case of drugs such as anabolic steroids, informed consent can be implied. Labeling laws or requirements for a doctor's prescription serve as a form of informed consent. The law presumes that people taking a prescription drug are aware of potentially negative side effects.

Informed consent solves certain philosophical problems associated with drug use. It does not significantly limit human freedom. It removes the problem of steroids from the realm of legal enforcement and returns it to the world of education and public opinion. American society can still express concern and opinions about people's moral lives but would not be able to punish people or risk creating a socially repressive atmosphere.

Of course, the same argument would work for any drug, even those such as heroin with well-documented negative effects. It also presumes consent can be informed and truly voluntary. However, steroids have the potential to be psychologically addicting. This calls into question whether people who become addicted can actually make a free and rational choice.

American society and culture value independence and encourage people to make the important choices that affect their own lives. Steroid users believe that if the choice to use steroids is informed and voluntary, and that choice is restricted, the law is denying people the values of self-reliance, personal achievement, and autonomy.

Decriminalizing steroids would solve this problem. For example, many elite athletes exhibit over-the-top dedication and determination. World-record holder Tim Montgomery, later revealed as an anabolic steroids user, said that if he won the gold medal at the Olympics, "it would not matter if I died on the other side of the finish line." Society might view this opinion as bizarre, insane, or just plain wrong, but it is hard to portray Montgomery as a deceived child.

On the other hand, the argument based on personal autonomy is at heart no different from the libertarian argument that has already been discredited. It presents the world in a stark either/or light; either the government must ban all bad things or it must allow them all. It seems ridiculous to say that if the government intervenes in even the slightest way, such as a law against jaywalking, the result will be tyranny and dictatorship. This position, while internally consistent, has little bearing on the real world. Some things do cause harm and many people genuinely believe it is their moral responsibility to prevent that damage if they can do so.

Cigarettes, Alcohol, and Cosmetic Surgery

If health concerns are the main reason for banning anabolic steroids, then many other things should probably be banned in America. Any argument supporting the restriction of steroids has to deal with the problems of cigarettes, alcohol, and cosmetic surgery. All these activities are more dangerous than using steroids.

For example, cigarettes are far more addictive than steroids. About 20 percent of all American adults (45 million people) smoke more than 350 billion cigarettes a year in the United States. Yet smokers are not subject to arrest and criminal prosecution even though the adverse health effects from cigarette smoking cause an estimated 438,000 deaths, or nearly one of every five deaths each year in the United States. In many places, smokers harm others with secondhand smoke. Each year, exposure to secondhand smoke causes 150,000 to 300,000 new cases of bronchitis and pneumonia in American children aged less than eighteen months.

Drinking alcohol is another minimally regulated activity. It is legal for everyone over age twenty-one even though alcohol abuse is a major problem in the United States. About 5 percent of Americans drink heavily and another 15 percent of the population binge drink. Binge drinking is the act of drinking many alcoholic beverages in a short time for the sole purpose of becoming drunk. From 2001 to 2005, excessive alcohol consumption caused about 75,000 deaths each year. In 2005 alone, there were more than 1.6 million hospitalizations and over 4 million emergency room visits for alcohol-related conditions. More than one-third of all automobile accidents in the United States are caused by alcohol consumption; about 15,000 Americans die every year from drunk driving. Alcohol was illegal in the United States from 1920 to 1933. However, most people concede that restricting alcohol consumption was a failure. Prohibition reduced alcohol consumption, but at the cost of a flourishing black market, increased crime, and widespread disrespect for the law.

The United States is a society preoccupied with physical appearance and self-image. Many steroid users are not competitive athletes but cosmetic users who want a "better body." The issue here is not cheating; steroids make them look and feel better in a way similar to using diet pills or undergoing liposuction. It is legal to perform operations to implant foreign prosthetics into almost all parts of the human body in order to satisfy people's desire to "look better." In these surgeries, patients face potentially fatal risks associated with general anesthesia and infection. More people have died or been permanently injured from botched cosmetic surgery procedures in the past few years than in nearly fifty years of anabolic steroid use by athletes. Although the risks of cosmetic surgery are unnecessary, the government does not forbid this activity. Yet doctors cannot legally prescribe anabolic steroids to a healthy, informed, consenting adult for cosmetic reasons.

As powerful as this argument seems, it remains as rigid as the one supporting informed consent. Just because some "bad" things are allowed by the law, it does not logically follow that all "bad"

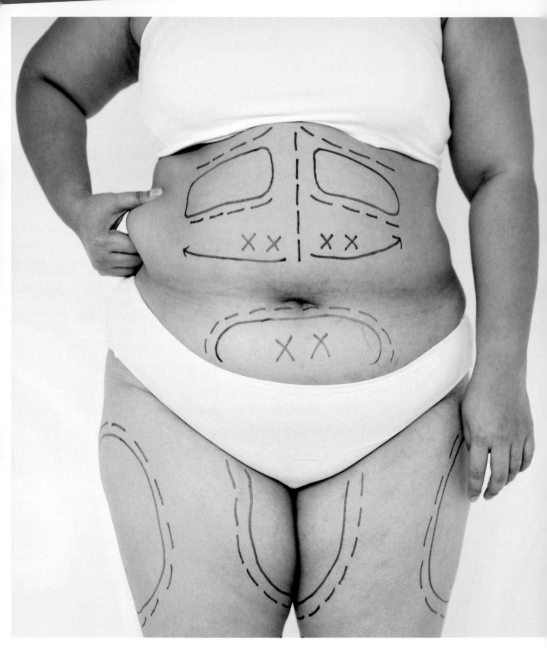

"It's better to look good than to feel good," in the words of a famous character on *Saturday Night Live*. Many, of course, seem to believe that to look good *is* to feel good, which may account for the raging popularity of liposuction, cosmetic surgery, and breast implants among the general population.

things must be allowed. The real world is complex, a product of compromises by competing interest groups. The legality of cigarettes might contradict the argument from harm but does not in itself make a case for the legality of nonmedical use of anabolic steroids. One might just as easily contend that society made a mistake in legalizing cigarettes. The habit is now too widespread (and too addictive) to eradicate by legislation. However, why should the same mistake be made repeatedly for the sake of total consistency?

It is a fallacy to insist that if people cannot find the perfect place to draw the line, then no line should be drawn at all. Democratic governments have to decide between those who are mature enough to vote and those who are not. There is nothing wrong with attempting to draw a reasonable line in good faith (e.g., an eighteen-year-old voting age) even if it is not perfect or appropriate for every person. In the same way, a reasonable attempt to prevent harm by making some drugs illegal is not automatically illogical.

Drug Testing and the T/E Ratio

If anabolic steroids are illegal, how will law enforcement agencies determine if people are using them? They might apprehend people in the act of using steroids or find witnesses to testify that someone did use them. Currently however, the most common way by far is through drug testing. Most people think drug testing as mainly taking place in sports, but it is also becoming increasingly common in schools and at places of employment. The concept of drug testing seems rather straightforward, but the issue becomes more complicated when a fine, loss of employment, and possible prison sentence depend on the outcome.

Testing for steroids and other drugs began in sports in the 1960s in response to several high-profile deaths attributed to amphetamine use. Drug tests quickly became a common feature of all major sporting events. Medical committees used urine samples to test for any of the substances featured on the IOC's banned list.

If a competitor failed to give a urine sample, the result was (and is) considered positive and that competitor might face severe penalties. Until the 1970s, there was no cost-effective way to screen urine samples for anabolic steroids. Because testosterone occurs naturally in the human body, it was difficult to distinguish between naturally produced and administered testosterone.

In 1982, scientists proposed that the ratio of testosterone (T) to epitestosterone (E) in urine might serve as a test for anabolic steroid use. The normal ratio of T/E in the human body is about 1:1. Within the body, there is little or no conversion of T to E or vice versa. If an athlete takes T, then the urine concentration of T rises for a short period while E does not. This elevated T/E ratio served as the starting point for the original IOC detection test for anabolic steroids. The IOC defined a positive test for testosterone abuse to be any T/E ratio of greater than 6:1.

Fear of legal challenges later forced the IOC to change its definition of a positive test. If a person's T/E ratio exceeded a 4:1 ratio, testers used extremely sophisticated carbon isotope ratio testing to determine whether the testosterone in an athlete's system was natural or synthetic. The additional testing is time-consuming and expensive and now takes place entirely for elite athletes in major competitions.

Screening procedures for anabolic steroids has become increasingly complex. The equipment costs several hundred thousand dollars and few hospitals and local medical labs can afford it. It costs anywhere from $50 to $250 per test for collecting, storing, and shipping the samples, and the laboratories might charge another $100 for analyzing the samples. Drug testing at the Beijing Summer Olympics of 2008 cost millions of dollars. The IOC has estimated that testing 100,000 potential Olympic athletes around the world once a year would cost about $30 million. Opponents of drug testing argue that this money would be better spent paying for health education programs.

Drug Testing and the Right to Privacy

Drug testing gradually moved from athletics to the office and the classroom. School boards and employers began to administer drug tests on a regular basis. Yet, on the surface, random drug testing appears to violate the U.S. Constitution. The Fourth Amendment declares that, "the right of the people to be secure in their persons, houses, papers and effects, against unreasonable searches and seizures shall not be violated." In addition, the Fourth Amendment states that "no warrants shall issue, but upon probable cause, supported by oath or affirmation, and particularly describing the place to be searched, and the persons or things to be seized."

Random urinalysis seems to intrude upon a person's supposed right to privacy in two ways. First, the subject is often monitored while providing the actual sample, and second, the test discloses personal information about the state of the subject's body and any materials she or he has ingested. In addition, random drug testing by definition means there is no particular suspicion of use. This seems to violate the right of people to be secure against unreasonable searches.

However, almost all sporting organizations now perform random mandatory drug testing based on urinalysis and this has withstood challenges on both federal and state constitutional grounds. U.S. courts have ruled that participating in an athletic event sponsored by a private sports association is not a right, but a privilege. Traditionally, courts have given private organizations (such as private employers or sports' governing bodies) very wide authority to define their own rights of membership.

Drug Testing and the U.S. Supreme Court

Governmental drug testing is not so clear-cut. To be reasonable under the Fourth Amendment, a search ordinarily must be based on individualized suspicion of wrongdoing. However, exceptions to this rule are sometimes granted based on "special needs, beyond the normal need for law enforcement."

The courts have consistently ruled that urinalysis is, in fact, a search. However, the U.S. Supreme Court in *Skinner* v. *Railway Labor Executives' Association* (1989) declared that random drug testing of certain railroad employees in "safety sensitive" positions was constitutional. In *Skinner*, the Court said that the privacy rights of employees were not as important as public safety. The same year, in *National Treasury Employees Union* v. *Von Raab*, the Supreme Court permitted the government to test customs officials who searched for drugs and firearms. Once again, the Court held that important national interests outweighed government workers' privacy expectations under the Fourth Amendment.

However, the Supreme Court has not given a blank check to random drug testing by governments. In two more recent cases, the Court set limits to drug testing. In *Chandler* v. *Miller* (1997), the Court struck down a Georgia law requiring political candidates for certain state offices to certify they had taken a drug test and that the result was negative. The Court noted Georgia had no evidence of a drug problem among elected officials and that those officials usually did not perform high-risk or safety-sensitive tasks. Therefore, the justices said that where "public safety is not genuinely in jeopardy, the Fourth Amendment precludes the suspicionless search, no matter how conveniently arranged."

In *Ferguson* v. *City of Charleston* (2001), the Supreme Court struck down a drug test imposed on pregnant women in city hospitals. In a 6-to-3 decision, the justices ruled that the typical patient taking diagnostic tests at a hospital could reasonably expect that the hospital would not share the results of those tests with nonmedical personnel without his or her consent. Instead, Charleston hospitals had turned over the results of these drug tests to the police without the women's consent. The justices complained that Charleston seemed to believe "virtually any nonconsensual suspicionless search could be immunized under the special needs doctrine by defining the search solely in terms of its ultimate . . . purpose." However, the discovery of wrongdoing does not in itself justify the search or make it legal. The constitutionality of particular drug tests remains a controversial aspect of the steroids question.

False Positives and Negatives

Drug testing accuracy is another controversial issue, especially for anabolic steroid use. Most medical research is concerned with disease prevention and treatment, not what a person has ingested to improve his or her performance or looks. Beginning in the 1970s, an entire drug-testing industry was created around the need to identify the substances in a person's urine. For some labs, drug testing can be extremely profitable, bringing in millions of dollars a year.

Urinalysis has its limitations even when performed perfectly. However, it is often not performed perfectly. Labs make mistakes despite careful protocols to make sure machines do not fail and humans do not make errors. Yet even though a positive test can destroy a career, labs often are not strictly liable for the failure of their procedures.

For example, when Floyd Landis was stripped of his Tour de France title in 2007, the shoddy work of some drug-testing labs became common knowledge. There were major record-keeping inconsistencies. Data were entered incorrectly and sometimes changed without authorization. Wide variations existed from one drug test to another. The recorded lab results did not always match up with the anonymous samples. Most shockingly, the lab technicians did not always know how to use their instruments. They had very little training and learned how to use the machines from their coworkers. Yet this was a lab paid to perform drug testing on one of the highest profile sporting events in the world. What then, could lab work be like for typical drug testing for a high school's football team?

Another problem is that drug testing for anabolic steroid use is extremely difficult. At best, sophisticated urine tests can only detect recent use in some people some of the time. And no test exists (as of 2009) for discovering if a person has used steroids at any previous time in their life. People can build their bodies using steroids for many months or even years. Then they can stop for a month or so and drug tests will certify that they had never used these drugs. Ultimately, the decision to use or not use steroids has a more solid base if it rests upon personal morals rather than the fear of drug testing.

Careful steroid users have access to specific guidelines, tables, and timetable methods to avoid detection. The information is easy enough to find from various sources, including the Internet. People can also use masking or disguising agents or techniques to avoid detection. Other deceptions include catheterization of urine, urine sample substitution, and urine sample manipulation. Some performance-enhancing substances, such as HGH, cannot be detected by a urine test at all as of 2009.

Current tests for anabolic steroids have other problems. The T/E ratio of 6:1 (or even 4:1) was an arbitrary number almost picked out of a hat. The high threshold was needed to avoid legal challenges, but tests that reveal a T/E ratio of less than 4:1 do not rule out recent steroid use. A lab will call it negative, but it may be a false negative. There is also debate whether the T/E ratio test is even valid for women; the aging process, menstruation, and the use of birth control pills can affect their level of testosterone.

In addition, anti-doping authorities have not clearly explained how they arrived at the criteria used to determine whether a drug test result is positive. The threshold for a positive result is often based on a very small number of volunteers taking the substance in question. Many people testing positive have vigorously denied using steroids. Some were lying, but for others, it has been nearly impossible for them to clear their names.

Nandrolone and the Ambiguity of Testing

Nandrolone is an anabolic steroid that may be present naturally in the human body in very small quantities. Nandrolone is sometimes used in the treatment of osteoporosis in older women. The drug can be detected indirectly in urine tests.

Nandrolone use by athletes, however, has caused a great deal of controversy. Several famous athletes have been banned from competition after failing tests for the steroid, including Marion Jones (U.S. sprinter), C. J. Hunter (U.S. shot putter), Linford Christie (British sprinter), Merlene Ottey (Jamaican two-hundred-meter world champion), and Dieter Baumann (German five-hundred-meter runner). After protesting their innocence, all were cleared by their national athletics organizations. However, Hunter and Jones later admitted they did, in fact, take the drug. Soccer stars Christophe Dugarry and Edgar Davids also tested positive for nandrolone, as did Czech tennis player Petr Korda.

Some people believe that the testing procedure for nandrolone may be flawed or inaccurate; surely so many people would not test positive for the same substance in such a short space of time. However, others suspect that the use of nandrolone is widespread. They speculate that other accused athletes, like Jones and Hunter, actually took the drug but continue to deny it as long as they can.

Blood and Hair Testing

Most drug testing is performed on a subject's urine samples. Many medical scientists have suggested the use of blood testing to detect anabolic steroid use. There are many advantages to testing blood instead of urine, including fewer false negatives and false positives.

However, there are problems with blood testing. Urine sampling is not invasive and a needle is not required. Some cultures do not accept or permit the drawing of blood. Urine testing produces less anxiety than blood testing and avoids any possibility of spreading needle-borne diseases. If a subject should contract a disease, then the organization performing the tests could be legally liable for millions of dollars in damages.

Blood testing for anabolic steroids is rare in the general population but is spreading in athletics. As of 2009, the most accurate EPO testing is also based on blood tests. There is no urine test for HGH; it can only be found with a blood test. However, American sports leagues such as the NFL and MLB have resisted blood testing. The players resent the presumed invasion of privacy and question the reliability of the tests. Despite testing seven hundred athletes at the 2004 Olympics in Athens and the 2008 Olympics in Beijing, anti-doping officials did not catch a single person using HGH.

Testing hair samples is another possible avenue of checking for anabolic steroids. In urine samples, evidence of steroid use is "washed out" within days. However, hair samples hold traces of drugs much longer. In 2008, a French anti-doping agency tested hair samples from 138 professional athletes and reported that twenty-two of them tested positive for some form of a banned drug.

Yet most experts do not currently consider hair testing reliable enough, particularly for testosterone, to use as legal evidence. There is a much greater risk of external contamination with hair than from blood and urine. As of 2009, testing of hair samples is allowed under French law but is not recognized by the World Anti-Doping Agency or cycling's governing body.

Here, a researcher prepares a hair sample from a suspected drug abuser for forensic analysis.

Biological Passports

A biological passport is a record of an individual's biological attributes developed over time from several sample collections. The passport creates a baseline report from the results of urine and blood tests. This type of testing is more relevant to athletics but there is no reason it could not be used for students or workers in the future.

The biological passport allows drug testers to see if there are changes from a person's baseline test that might indicate drug use. The advantage of a biological passport is that testers do not need to know every possible type of anabolic steroid; they look only for an indication that something is being used even if the specific drug remains unknown. The International Cycling Union (UCI) began a blood profile program in 2008. The UCI collected an average of ten samples each from more than eight hundred cyclists in random drug tests, both in and out of competition.

Obviously, the use of a biological passport raises serious privacy issues. There are the usual objections about the invasiveness of drawing blood. In addition, any private or governmental organization with these records would own some of the most intimate details of a person's life. There are also due process issues. Should a person be judged guilty of using drugs without any physical evidence that a drug was used? After all, a change in a person's baseline would not provide direct evidence that a person took a prohibited drug. It would be difficult to take punitive action against an individual based on a change in a biological profile without specific evidence a person was using a prohibited substance.

Adolescents and Drug Testing

Doctors and scientists agree that adolescent anabolic steroid users face special dangers, such as stunted growth and greater risk of injury. There is little controversy that adolescents should not be allowed to take steroids. It is accepted legal practice that individuals under a certain age lack the reasoning power to give an informed consent. American law forbids minors from certain positive actions (voting), value-free actions (driving a car), and negative actions (smoking cigarettes) until they reach a certain age.

The right of the government to test adolescents for drugs is not quite as clear. Voting, smoking, and driving are actions that take place outside the school. However, drug testing usually takes place within a school setting and may involve random and mandatory tests. In *Tinker* v. *Des Moines* (1969), a free speech case, the U.S. Supreme Court wrote, "It can hardly be argued that either students or teachers shed their constitutional rights...at the schoolhouse gate." Yet the Supreme Court has also held that the rights of students inside a school are not the same as rights of adults outside of school. In *New Jersey* v. *TLO* (1985), the Court stated that schools must balance a student's legitimate expectation of privacy and the school's interest in maintaining order. Therefore, school officials did not need a warrant to search students' belongings if they had a "reasonable suspicion" that an individual had drugs.

Though teens who oppose drug testing have taken their cases to the Supreme Court, the teens have remained on the losing side of the argument. Christian Balden, a high school student in Oklahoma who opposes drug testing, talks to a campus security officer. His flyers explained his position but did not persuade the school authorities to change policy.

But random drug tests do not involve individualized "reasonable suspicion." Do students have the right to refuse one? One Oregon school district required student athletes to submit to random drug testing before being allowed to participate in high school sports. In *Vernonia School District 47J* v. *Acton* (1995), the Supreme Court ruled that although the drug tests were searches under the Fourth Amendment, they were reasonable searches because the school had an interest in preventing teenage drug use. Therefore, mandatory random drug testing for student athletes was constitutional.

In *Board of Education* [Tecumseh, OK] v. *Earls* (2002), the Supreme Court expanded the *Vernonia* ruling and allowed schools to drug test all students who participated in extracurricular activities. By a 5-to-4 margin, the Court ruled that students in extracurricular activities had diminished expectations of privacy and that the school had an important interest in preventing drug use. Therefore, students had to consent to random urinalysis in order to sing in the chorus or join the chess club.

Thus, the Supreme Court in the last forty years has kept increasing the power of schools to test for drugs. The next step would seemingly be to give schools the right to mandatory testing of the entire student body for drugs.

However, efforts to test high school students for steroids are losing steam, not for legal reasons but due to high costs and the lack of positive results. New Jersey, Florida, Texas, and Illinois all tested random students between 2006 and 2009, and only eighteen tests out of 30,799 came back positive. Florida dropped its program in 2008 after an expensive one-year trial in which there was only one positive out of six hundred tests. For whatever reason, those results are far short of surveys that found 2.2 percent of seniors said they had tried steroids at least once. It is hard for schools to justify spending up to two hundred dollars per test for tests that rarely catch cheaters.

5 Athletic Issues: Cheating and Sports

Is Cheating Wrong?

Although the majority of anabolic steroid users are not elite athletes, the controversy over steroid use often takes place in the world of sports. Drug bans and drug testing are meant not only to protect people from harm but also to preserve the concept of fair play.

However, "sports" is a word, like "love," that is particularly hard to define. Modern sports seem to refer simultaneously to the pleasant diversion of play and to intensely competitive athletic contests. In general, sports seem to require competition, which may or may not include kayaking, throwing a Frisbee, and running.

If sports is a difficult word to define, then its purpose is even more vague. Is it to develop character? To socialize players into society? To teach the importance of competition? To entertain the masses? Is it simply a business, like selling lemonade and lending money? Does it even have a "purpose"?

There seems to be no "true" definition of sporting ideals for all times and all places. Each society and culture constructs its own value system and projects it onto athletic contests. This makes it very difficult to argue about the appropriateness of anabolic steroid use in sports. Without a universally accepted conception of the nature of sports, the use of performance-enhancing drugs is open to controversy between people who hold competing definitions.

"Cheating" is also a hard concept to define. Most people think of cheating as an act of lying, deception, or trickery used to create an unfair advantage. In sports, cheating implies breaking rules that were implicitly agreed upon when teams or people agreed to compete. In this view, steroid use is a form of cheating because it contradicts the concept that sports should be about fair play and equal opportunity.

Americans view cheating as unacceptable behavior yet it is important to remember that cheating is common in American society. Some of the most successful people in the United States cut corners to achieve fame and fortune. In theory, people who cheat risk punishment. However, in many cases, people perceive that the punishment does not fit the crime. For cheaters who do get caught, such as white-collar thieves, the punishment is often very light.

Capitalism emphasizes winning and individual self-interest. When Americans weigh the rewards of cheating against the drawbacks, many choose the former. They balance the idea that integrity is an asset in life with the knowledge that successful cheating can advance one's self-interest, especially if "everybody else" is doing it. The American cultural climate emphasizes a competitive winner-take-all philosophy that leads to law enforcement personnel who lie, business leaders who fix the books, academics who plagiarize, doctors who fabricate bills, and journalists who make up stories. Many people in these professions are honest and cheaters may be an exception. However, it is clear that proper moral behavior is not always rewarded in American society and improper behavior is often neither detected nor punished when it is.

Teenagers are particularly ambivalent about cheating. In a 2004 poll of 30,000 high school students, 59 percent agreed that "successful people do what they have to do to win, even if others consider it cheating." In that year, 30 percent of the students admitted to having stolen from a store, 64 percent had cheated on a test, and 36 percent used the Internet to plagiarize an assignment. Despite these responses, 93 percent of the students said they were satisfied with their personal ethics and character and 77 percent agreed with the statement that "when it comes to doing what is right, I am better than most people I know." In justifying cheating, one student said, "Good grades can make the difference between going to medical school and being a janitor." If all that matters is the individual's "bottom line," then this argument has considerable force.

"If the Ref Doesn't See It . . . "

Cheating in sports is easier to define in theory than in practice. Oftentimes, the moral concept of "cheating" depends on the time, the place, and the situation. Sports might have rule books but these rules are paper commandments only. Cheating may "unfairly" further the cheater's self-interest but, at a safe distance, many cultures enjoy the wit and audacity of successful liars. Many of the heroes of mythology and the Bible win by trickery or by help from an external force. The cheater (or trickster) who outwits others through outright fraud is often a cultural hero.

In sports, the rule book cannot possibly eliminate all ambiguity. Athletes are taught from a young age to "bend" the rules. Many have heard their coaches tell them, "If you're not cheating, you're not trying." A basic maxim of modern American athletics is that "if the ref didn't see it, it's not a foul." Soccer players learn to "dive" to win penalties. Basketball players learn to "flop" to draw a charging foul. Football players are often coached to use illegal techniques to hold or trip opponents without detection. Many prestigious American colleges have been penalized for recruiting violations. Sports are supposed to "build character" but dishonesty in sports is not always viewed as a morally reprehensible act.

For example, the sport of baseball has a rich tradition of bent and broken rules. Coaches steal signs, runners go out of the base paths to break up double plays, ground crews water down fields to slow the ball, catchers scuff up baseballs to benefit pitchers. Gaylord Perry, a baseball pitcher famous for (admittedly) throwing

Amateurs and Professionals

Pierre de Coubertin, the Frenchman who founded the modern Olympic movement in the 1890s, was a romantic idealist. He believed sports could bring people from different nations together and promote peace through healthy competition. This was the view of the European and American upper classes at the time. They thought the purpose of sports was to teach discipline, cooperation, and sacrifice. According to this view, true "sportsmen" were amateurs. An amateur is a person who does something without pay or formal training. The word comes from the Latin *amator*, meaning lover or devoted friend. Amateur sportsmen played simply for the love of the sport.

Yet by the late 1800s, sports like baseball, cycling, rowing, and soccer had professional players. A professional is a person who receives training in a particular activity and makes a living from it. Working–class men at the turn of the century realized that excellence in sports could lead to fame, higher status, and, most importantly, could provide a career for successful competitors.

Amateurs and professionals have had an uneasy relationship for more than a century. However, professionals have won the verbal battle. The word "amateur" now implies someone lacking professional skills or expertise. To call someone an amateur is usually an insult. An amateur might try very hard at something but is not particularly good at it. On the other hand, the adjective "professional" sometimes has negative connotations; professionals are perhaps a bit too cynical and perform more for money than out of passion.

If you win and get away with it, is it cheating? Giants player Barry Bonds, under investigation for perjury concerning earlier steroid use, is greeted warmly by Los Angeles Dodgers coach Mariano Duncan.

illegal spitballs, was elected to the Hall of Fame. Yet all of these things are considered by most fans to be "part of the game." If they are part of the game, are they cheating?

One might argue that baseball players expect their opponents to use these strategies to gain an advantage even though they might be against the rules. All sorts of subtle illegalities have become part of many different games. The judgment of what is and is not cheating is not always clear-cut. Somewhere along the line, it became expected in baseball to try to break certain rules but not others.

To a degree, this explanation begs the question: Who decided (and when) that it was acceptable to break some rules? No vote was ever taken and the rule book still exists. Yet players and fans seem to be in general agreement in most sports of what constitutes cheating. They base their judgment on vague appeals to their own wisdom, experience, and the traditions of the game.

In the matter of anabolic steroids, however, sporting wisdom and tradition provide few answers. Before the 1960s, there was no public scandal relating to drug use in sports and there was no sustained campaign against it. Athletes, spectators, and sports governing bodies accepted everyday use of amphetamines in cycling, soccer, and rowing. Very few people raised the idea that drugs contradicted the ideals of fair play. In 1965, one writer commented, "The use of a substance or device which improves a man's physical performance without being injurious to his health, can hardly be called unethical. . . . As for taking advantage of other contestants who do not use these aids, this should be regarded in the same light as the use of special diets, massage, special exercises, and so forth."

Five-time Tour de France winner Jacques Anquetil argued in the 1960s that professional cyclists should be allowed to take drugs. He argued that professional riders were workers and had the same right to treat their pains as a geography teacher. In 1965, he declared, "Everyone in cycling dopes himself. Those who claim they don't are liars." If everyone took drugs, then was it an acceptable form of rule breaking?

In addition, the concept of unfair advantage is a relative idea. Some people, and some nations, are rich or poor. Access to elite coaches, sophisticated equipment, the latest training techniques, and knowledgeable sports scientists also give advantages to those without such luxuries. One could go as far as claiming that genetic endowment in general is an unfair advantage. The basketball player, Yao Ming, is 7' 6" tall. Usain Bolt ran two hundred meters in 22.04 seconds as a fifteen-year-old.

"Cheat or Lose"

In some sports, there is a disconnect between the participants and their fans. Many fans yearn for drug-free performances and condemn athletes who use steroids. They feel that if the rules of a sport forbid the use of a substance and a player knowingly takes it, then he or she is a cheater by definition and deserves punishment. The problem of steroids shakes the faith of many fans in the fairness of the contest they are watching and in the records achieved.

Yet athletes who use performance-enhancing substances have turned the argument of "a level playing field" on its head. Charles Francis, Ben Johnson's coach, declared that steroid abuse was so pervasive in Olympic sports it was impossible to succeed without drugs. Francis admitted he had provided drugs to Johnson, but insisted, "We had no reason to believe that anyone at the highest levels was not using performance-enhancing drugs." It was a simple case of cheat or lose.

The same line was taken by baseball star Ken Caminiti. He said, "At first I felt like a cheater. But I looked around, and everybody was doing it." Caminiti claimed, "If a young player were to ask me what to do, I'm not going to tell him [steroids] are bad. . . . I can't say, 'Don't do it,' not when the guy next to you is as big as a house and he's going to take your job and make the money."

California physician Robert Kerr admitted to prescribing steroids for four thousand patients, many of them celebrities and Olympic medal winners. When asked on national television about the ethics of helping athletes cheat, Kerr responded, "This is not cheating—not when everyone does it."

According to this argument, taking steroids was like stealing signs in baseball. It may be against the rules but is an accepted part of the game acknowledged by all the players, if not by all fans. Steroid users believe it is a fair competitive environment if all athletes competing in a sport decide to use anabolic steroids. But what if some players do not want to use anabolic steroids?

The Argument of the Coercion of Athletes

Earlier, the argument that anabolic steroid use harms the people taking the drugs was discussed. However, a powerful argument can be made that steroid use hurts other people, specifically athletes who are pressured to take it against their will in order to compete— similar to the way Judy Garland was forced to take amphetamines to control her weight when she was a teenage actress. Steroid use opponents argue that they are simply concerned with athletes' health and the desire to avoid a situation in elite sports where all athletes are taking unnecessary risks with their lives. Hundreds of elite athletes have complained that they are forced to use steroids in order to compete against other top athletes who are also using drugs. Permitting steroid users to compete with drug-free athletes affects the fairness of every level of athletic competition.

Professional sports are an extreme environment. Success can make an athlete rich and famous while failure can leave the same person injured, broke, and unemployed. People act in extreme ways with such high stakes. Elite athletes take drugs because they are hyper-competitive but also because their livelihood depends on success.

Faced with competitors who use anabolic steroids, other athletes have only a few alternatives. They can:

1. compete without steroids, knowing that they may lose to competitors who do not follow the rules
2. abandon the sport because they do not want to use steroids
3. use steroids to level the playing field

In this way, anabolic steroids expose elite athletes to health risks, whether serious or not. Some athletes feel compelled to use steroids and therefore run medical risks they otherwise would not choose to run.

The problem with this argument is that all competitive pressure becomes "coercive." Steroid users argue that elite sport is already a coercive environment. When full-time training, altitude training, weight training, or diet control were shown to produce better results, all competitors were forced to adopt these measures to keep up. Is steroid use really more coercive than training eight hours a day? No one is forced to become a competitive athlete.

Of course, this rebuttal hinges on the idea that steroid use is not particularly harmful. However, some athletes believe they are being coerced into significant risks with their health by using steroids. And if "safe and effective" anabolic steroids actually existed, would athletes use dosages within their therapeutic range? Competitive athletes rarely know when to stop; they would probably keep increasing the dosage in order to gain advantages over competitors. Yet most substances are toxic if taken in large enough amounts.

Steroid users point out that these ethical dilemmas are not unique to sports. There are risks to joining the military, flying an airplane, or researching a disease. In the end, the final choice still rests with the individual. The acceptability of the argument depends on the way "coercion" is defined.

Athletes as Role Models

Young people in the United States look up to athletes as role models. If elite athletes take steroids, they are no longer suitable as role models and the public has lost a significant benefit. This is a form of harm to others. California governor Arnold Schwarzenegger said in 2009, "I think it's important to get the message out that we should not use drugs. I think we have a certain obligation as athletes to inspire young people. When someone wins an Olympic championship or a boxing championship, whatever it may be, you're not only a champion, but you're also an inspirational vehicle for young kids and for people in general to stay fit [and] to lose weight. . . . "

Children see athletes take drugs and have no respect for the rules of the game. In one study, more than half of adolescents believed "it is common for famous athletes to use steroids or other banned substances in order to get an edge on the competition." If athletes send the message that illegal steroid use is acceptable, more young people will use these substances to copy famous figures. And they may also get the message that it is acceptable to cheat in other areas as well.

For example, the baseball superstar Mark McGwire admitted to using andro in 1998. In the next year, sales of that (then-legal) steroid precursor increased by more than 1,000 percent. McGwire may not have wanted to be a role model, but he was one. By 2001, 8 percent of male high school seniors had used andro during the prior year. On the other hand, why should sports figures be role models? They did not sign up for the position. Americans do not expect popular musicians or actors to serve as perfect models for teenagers. Nonetheless, supporters of a steroid ban argue that perhaps famous athletes should not be role models, but the reality is that they are heroes for many people. The law has to deal with the way things are and not the way things should be in theory.

There is still the philosophical question of evaluating steroid use by athletes before it was banned. In the 1960s, there were no laws against steroids and few doctors raised serious health concerns. California governor Arnold Schwarzenegger admitted that he used steroids in the 1970s to win bodybuilding titles and become world famous. Was he a drug cheat and undeserving of being a role model?

Harold Connolly was an American athlete who won the gold medal in the hammer throw at the 1956 Olympic Games. His left arm was damaged at birth and he spent his youth in physical therapy, working tirelessly on strength conditioning. He set the American record twelve times and the world record seven times. A statue of Connolly commemorating his accomplishments stands in

Boston. Yet Connolly freely admits he used steroids (as did almost all hammer throwers of the time) to set these records. If the act of taking steroids is unethical in itself, then Connolly should have known better and should be condemned as a cheat. If the illegality of steroids is the principal objection, then Connolly's statue is entirely justified since steroid use was legal at the time.

Fans show their support for New York Yankees third baseman Alex Rodriguez. They are unconcerned about allegations of steroid abuse.

Unnatural vs. Natural

Opponents of anabolic steroids claim that sports should be a function of factors internal to the athletes, such as intelligence, motivation, courage, and genes. They argue that steroids are an external factor and therefore unnatural. Drug-enhanced performance doesn't come from an athlete's personal qualities or strengths. Instead, the performance comes from a person's ability to best use the steroid's potential benefits to perform beyond natural human limits. According to this view, steroids should be banned because they destroy the true concept of sports even if all participants use them and agree to allow their use. The use of steroids represents a perversion of sports. It converts the beauty of athletics—the thrill of victory, the agony of defeat, the striving and achieving—into biotechnology.

If athletes depend on drugs for their performance, then chemists will ultimately determine the outcome of sporting events. For example, Ken Patera, an American weightlifting champion from the 1970s, looked forward to meeting the Russian champion in the Olympics. He said, "Last year the only difference between me and him was I couldn't afford his drug bill. Now I can. When I hit Munich, I'll weigh in at about 340, or maybe 350. Then we'll see which are better, his steroids or mine." Patera implied, rightly or wrongly, that the athletic contest would not be decided by who had best developed his or her skill or strength, but by the body that had taken the most effective drugs at the proper time and most productive dosage.

Although this argument has a certain amount of power, it runs into difficulty in trying to define "natural" and "unnatural." Is steroid use more of an advantage than access to elite equipment, coaching, and training? Medicine and drugs help athletes prevent and recover from injuries better than ever before. Even laboratory-engineered protein shakes, nutrition bars, and vitamin tablets theoretically violate notions of "natural" training. Yet few people claim these tools are ruining the competitive integrity of sport. Which of these is "unnatural": vitamins, caffeine pills, oxygen, amino acids, HGH, a sports drink, marijuana, or herbal tea? It is almost impossible to arrive at an accurate definition.

The same ambiguity appears when dealing with technological changes. The use of fiberglass poles, synthetic track surfaces, compound bows, and high-tech tennis rackets all seem unnatural but are allowed. Yet at the same time, corked bats or high-pressure golf balls are not allowed. The distinction is not very clear.

The fact that steroids are derived from a naturally produced hormone in the human body presents another problem. Athletes who use steroids claim they are simply supplementing what is already in their body. When athletes take large doses of painkillers, anti-inflammatories, or muscle relaxants to keep them playing through pain, they are honored as heroes. But if they take testosterone-based drugs to help them rebuild the muscles damaged by playing through injury, they are attacked as criminals and drug cheats. The idea that any drug-taking is wrong sets up an almost impossible situation.

The argument that sports should be "natural" is also complicated by the legal status of chemical sports supplements such as creatine. Americans spent more than $22.5 billion on nutritional supplements in 2006. Sports nutrition alone was a $2.4 billion industry in 2006. Some reports suggest that approximately 25 percent of professional baseball players and up to 50 percent of professional football players use creatine supplements. In 2003, creatine sales totaled $193 million, or about 10 percent of the sports supplement market.

The Problem of Due Process

Drug testing changed the face of modern sports. It cast the shadow of suspicion over all athletes. Urine and blood tests seem to provide a positive result at about one percent but the watching public "knows" that a much higher percentage have been found guilty.

Elite athletes depend on success in their sport to make money. An accusation of steroid use can ruin an athlete. It might mean a suspension or even force retirement. Yet lab technicians are only human and laboratories make mistakes. Tests might be performed incorrectly and samples mislabeled or contaminated. However, once an athlete faces a charge of providing a positive steroids test, the concept of "innocent until proven guilty" no longer applies.

Athletes can appeal to the court system of their respective countries in order to fight a doping accusation. However, the IOC and other international sporting bodies have disputed the right of athletes to challenge drug-testing procedures, results, and sanctions in national courts. The intervention of these courts would make it almost impossible to organize an international fight against steroids. National courts tend to favor athletes from their country. There are also different standards from country to country. The whole enforcement system would collapse if an athlete suspended for steroid use could obtain a court order reversing an IOC decision and allowing the athlete to compete until legal procedures were finished.

As a result, most international competitions require elite athletes to sign an arbitration agreement before competing. The Court of Arbitration for Sport (CAS) is the international arbitration body created in 1984 to settle disputes related to sports. The CAS originally dealt with disputes during the Olympics and, in its early years, was little more than an arm of the IOC. In 1994, a court case in Switzerland revealed these close links. As a result, the CAS agreed to several organizational and financial reforms to make it more independent of the IOC. As of 2009, almost every Olympic International Federation and National Olympic Committee has recognized the jurisdiction of the CAS and refers their arbitration disputes to it. Most CAS arbitration cases deal with transfer disputes in professional soccer or with doping.

However, athletes continue to complain about the CAS. Many athletes grumble that the court still favors the Olympics' management. They point out the people who select the arbitrators are often members of either the IOC or the Association of National Olympic Committees. This is a conflict of interest because those are the governing bodies usually bringing the charges of drug use against the athlete in the first place.

In addition, arbitration often has a short time frame that does not offer the athlete the same protections as a jury trial. Athletes want to make sure they receive due process: timely notification of a positive test, the opportunity for an athlete to appear, the chance to examine the necessary documentation from the lab and to cross-examine witnesses, and an appeals process for the correction of errors. At present, athletes can only argue that the lab performed the testing incorrectly or interpreted the data incorrectly; they cannot challenge test validity. As with any international court, there are also complaints about inconsistent penalties. Nonetheless, no one has suggested a workable alternative to the CAS that can resolve international sports-related disputes quickly and inexpensively.

A recent trend in the United States is to subpoena athletes to testify under oath about their personal habits in front of a congressional committee. Government officials justify these investigations in the name of "cleaning up sports" or some other vaguely defined "public interest." Athletes believe that the major private sporting bodies have their own rules and do not need Congress or federal prosecutors to act as their enforcers. However, these show hearings—so-called because they are, indeed, just for show—are likely to continue as long as anabolic steroid use is illegal and the majority of fans oppose its use.

Nonanalytical Positive

A nonanalytical positive is circumstantial evidence that an arbitration panel finds strong enough to rule that a drug violation took place. In 2004, Michelle Collins, an American sprinter, was banned from competition for eight years even though she had never failed an in- or out-of-competition steroids test. The U.S. Anti-Doping Agency (USADA) suspended Collins based on patterns observed in her blood and urine tests, as well as evidence from the BALCO investigation. Collins agreed to drop her appeal to the CAS in exchange for a four-year ban. She was the first athlete to be banned for a nonanalytical positive without a positive test or an admission of drug use. (She later admitted to taking steroids and was reinstated in 2008).

In 2005, the CAS upheld the suspensions of sprinters Tim Montgomery and Chryste Gaines for nonanalytical positives. Montgomery and Gaines, both tied to the BALCO case, had also never tested positive for drugs. Despite the lack of direct evidence, CAS decided there was enough indirect evidence to support their suspensions.

According to the USADA, prosecutors of an anti-steroids case must only prove a case to the "comfortable satisfaction" of the arbitration panel. This standard is far less rigorous than the normal standard of "beyond a reasonable doubt" of jury trials. For this reason, the "nonanalytical positive" raises questions about adequate "due process" protection for athletes. It is a powerful weapon to use against athletes because anti-doping groups no longer need physical evidence of steroids use. Instead, they can pursue doping cases based on accusations by someone who appears to be a credible witness.

It doesn't always take a drug test. American sprinter Michelle Collins was suspended from Olympic competition for eight years because of patterns observed in her blood and urine tests, even though she had never failed an actual test for steroids.

The Problem
of Varying
Standards

Randy Barnes was an American shot putter who, as of 2009, still holds the men's world indoor and outdoor distance records he set in 1989 and 1990. In 1990, Barnes was banned from competing for twenty-seven months after testing positive for anabolic steroids. Barnes argued that the drug sample was not his but the suspension stood and he missed the 1992 Olympics. However, at the 1996 Olympic Games, Barnes won the gold medal with a come-from-behind throw on his final attempt.

In 1998, Barnes tested positive for andro, the over-the-counter supplement famously used by Mark McGwire in his assault on the home run record. Andro was legal at the time and accepted in baseball. However, it was banned in track and field. Although Barnes claimed he did not know andro was banned, he was suspended from competition in the Olympic Games for life.

Randy Barnes received a lifetime ban for andro use; McGwire received millions of dollars and became an American hero. Both men were taking the same drug.

Creation of the World Anti-Doping Agency (WADA)

The problems with the CAS demonstrated how difficult it was to establish uniform standards in athletics. In some countries, an athlete could take a drug while other countries banned it. Sometimes, different sports in the same country had differing prohibited drug lists. However, only an anti-doping agency free from any control by the national sports federations or the IOC would be acceptable to athletes.

WADA was established in 1999 to coordinate the international fight against drugs in sports. It is supposedly an independent foundation but it was created mainly through the will of the IOC. As of 2007, WADA received about half its funding from the IOC and the other half from various national governments. WADA helps individual sporting federations implement testing procedures, perform research, and develop educational programs.

However, WADA is best known for producing a list of prohibited substances that athletes are not permitted to take. Sports organizations used the WADA Code for the first time in 2004 before the Athens Olympics. The WADA Code standardized the rules and regulations governing anti-doping across all sports and all countries. However, WADA's Code does not have the status of international law.

The WADA Code states that a substance on the prohibited list must meet two of the following three criteria:

1. It must be contrary to the spirit of sport.
2. It must be performance-enhancing.
3. It must be injurious to the health of the athlete.

Yet all of these standards are vague and open to interpretation. For example, marijuana is banned by WADA even though the organization admits it is not performance-enhancing. Instead, WADA claims the use of marijuana violates number one and

Excerpts from the WADA 2009 Prohibited List—World Anti-Doping Code

"Where an anabolic androgenic steroid is capable of being produced endogenously, a Sample will be deemed to contain such Prohibited Substance and an Adverse Analytical Finding will be reported where the concentration of such Prohibited Substance or its metabolites or markers and/or any other relevant ratio(s) in the Athlete's Sample so deviates from the range of values normally found in humans that it is unlikely to be consistent with normal endogenous production. A Sample shall not be deemed to contain a Prohibited Substance in any such case where an Athlete proves that the concentration of the Prohibited Substance or its metabolites or markers and/or the relevant ratio(s) in the Athlete's Sample is attributable to a physiological or pathological condition...

When a value does not so deviate from the range of values normally found in humans and any reliable analytical method (e.g. IRMS) has not determined the exogenous origin of the substance, but if there are indications, such as a comparison to endogenous reference steroid profiles, of a possible Use of a Prohibited Substance, or when a laboratory has reported a T/E ratio greater than four (4) to one (1) and any reliable analytical method (e.g. IRMS) has not determined the exogenous origin of the substance, further investigation shall be conducted by the relevant Anti-Doping Organization by reviewing the results of any previous test(s) or by conducting subsequent test(s)....

Should an Athlete fail to cooperate in the investigations, the Athlete's Sample shall be deemed to contain a Prohibited Substance."

number three, a position that many athletes dispute. Nor is there a convincing reason why two of the three criteria, rather than one or all of the criteria, must be met for a drug to be banned. Athletes who violate WADA's list are breaking the rules, but the deeper philosophical questions regarding anabolic steroid use remain unanswered.

The Whereabouts Issue

Olympic sports such as track and field, figure skating, and weightlifting have the strictest drug-testing policy in sports. Olympic athletes, unlike American baseball or football players, are not part of a strong union. They are totally at the mercy of the IOC, the governing body for the Olympics.

Olympic athletes face the likelihood of drug testing both during competitions and in training. They must file a document listing their whereabouts at all times of the year, even when on vacation. A tester seeking a urine sample can show up at an athlete's house, day or night, without warning. An athlete can be disqualified from competition for two years if caught just once and then banned for life if caught a second time.

In the United States, all Olympic athletes are subject to year-round testing by the USADA, which follows the WADA Code. Athletes must submit quarterly updates of home and training addresses. Unannounced, out-of-competition screening made up 61 percent of USADA tests in 2007.

WADA's anti-doping code originally required athletes to select one hour per day, five days a week, during which they were available for no-notice drug tests. However, in 2009, this was extended to seven days a week and, unlike the previous system, athletes must be available for the full day. This drew a legal challenge from the Belgian sports union, which argued that the system violates the European Convention on Human Rights. The Fédération Internationale de Football Association (FIFA), the governing body of international soccer, also challenged the invasion of privacy. FIFA believed soccer players should be available for testing only when they are in the stadium or the training complex. FIFA stated, "Both on a political and juridical level, the legality of the lack of respect of the private life of players, a fundamental element of individual liberty, can be questioned." Yet it is impossible for a steroids policy to be effective without no-notice, out-of-competition drug testing.

If an athlete fails to cooperate in the investigations, the athlete's sample is considered to contain a prohibited substance. For example, Konstantinos Kenteris was a Greek sprinter who won the gold medal in the two hundred meters at the 2000 Summer Olympics. In the 2004 Olympics at Athens, Kenteris was a popular favorite of the home crowd to win a gold medal. However, on the day before the games began, Kenteris failed to show up for a drug test. He claimed to have been injured in a motorcycle accident but an official Greek investigation would later find that the alleged accident had been staged. In the following scandal, Kenteris withdrew from the Olympics. In 2005, he was cleared of all charges by the Greek athletics federation. Five years later, the case is still dragging on in the courts.

Even beyond the philosophical question of anabolic steroid use, drug testing of athletes has many controversial aspects. These questions regarding privacy and due process are unlikely to be resolved to everyone's satisfaction in the near future.

Congress has convened many hearings on athletic steroid abuse. In 2007, Republican Senator Charles Grassley announced a set of proposals that would limit access to performance-enhancing drugs and attach criminal penalties to their distribution. The proposals have not been signed into law.

6 The Future Debate

Can Athletics Possibly Be Drug Free?

Human beings have taken a wide variety of everyday and exotic substances over the years, and drug use has never been limited to elite athletes. Yet the debate over anabolic steroid use usually focuses on sports. Former attorney general John Ashcroft said, "Illegal steroid use calls into question not only the integrity of the athletes who use them, but also the integrity of the sports that those athletes play. Steroids are bad for sports, they're bad for players, they're bad for young people who hold athletes up as role models." A famous sportswriter added, "Let's put the right word on it. Any player who took steroids is a fixer. He fixed games."

Yet physicians, pharmacists, chemists, inventors, and athletes continue to try to develop new and improved steroids and other performance-enhancing drugs. Americans use steroids because they can train harder, more intensively, and for longer periods. The governing bodies of each sport face a constant struggle to keep their tests accurate and up to date. Despite the threat of jail and reports of harmful side effects, Americans continue to use steroids to improve their performance, appearance, and ability to function in their occupation. It is a legitimate question whether it will ever be possible to have a drug-free environment.

Testing for anabolic steroids has become progressively more sophisticated but this only leads to greater efforts at masking steroid use. As soon as detection methods are developed for one anabolic steroid, elite athletes and drugmakers move on to another. Many of these new drugs are undetectable by current drug tests. The incentives for the athletes—fame and fortune—are much greater than the incentives for the testers. For example, one antidrug official admitted with a shrug that the biological passport system would be successful for "about a year or so until riders figure a way around it . . . we'll catch the least sophisticated ones. The others will be more careful."

An enforceable ban on steroids requires a complex bureaucracy to succeed: testers and monitors to detect drug use in and out of competition, scientists to evaluate the results of tests, and a judicial system to provide a place for appeal as well as to levy and enforce punishment. This is an extremely expensive and potentially intrusive system, and one that is completely unrelated to the sport in question. Facing these facts, some sports officials have thrown up their hands. Juan Samaranch, former president of the IOC, suggested reducing the number of banned drugs. He said, "Doping now is everything that, firstly, is harmful to an athlete's health and, secondly, artificially augments his performance. If it's just the second case, for me, that's not doping. If it's the first case, it is."

It seems unlikely that athletes will stop exploring ways to improve their performances with chemicals and drugs any time in the near future. Perhaps the most astonishing piece of evidence is a survey of 198 aspiring American Olympians in 1995. They were asked, "If you were offered a banned performance-enhancing substance with guarantees that you will not be caught and that you will win, would you take the substance?" Of the 198 athletes questioned, 195 answered that they would take the substance; only 3 said no. When the stipulation was added that, by taking the substance, they would win every competition for the next five years and then die from the effects of the substance, more than 60 percent still said yes.

World Records
in Track and
Field

Some of the world records in track and field, particularly women's sprinting and men's field events, have lasted more than twenty years. For example, the six fastest times in the women's four hundred meters all predate 1996. It is possible that the limits of human achievement have been reached. However, there also may be a correlation between the lack of new records and the advent of out–of–competition random anabolic steroids testing. On the one hand, this would show that drug tests do reduce steroid use. However, it also raises the question of what to do about the previous records.

Some people have argued that athletes who used steroids should be stripped of their records and medals. However, the logistics of doing this would be incredibly complex and the sports governing organizations have not been supportive. Others suggest that all world records should be eliminated and reset as of 2000 now that there is out-of-competition testing. Some support a dual standard of records for the years before and after the year 2000.

On the other hand, athletes who support steroid use complain that anti-doping efforts have led to the stagnation of records at the national, Olympic, and world levels. They believe this lack of world records hurts the sports business. Jim Doehring, the 1988 Olympic shot putter, admitted that he was a steroid user. He claimed that if track and field eliminated steroids, no one would watch. "It's going to be a dying sport if they finally clean it up. You'll have guys running the 100 in 11 flat, throwing the javelin 220 feet, throwing [the shot put] 65 feet. Who's going to come to see that?"

Jamaican athlete Melanie Walker, U.S. athlete Sheena Toster, and Ukraine's Anastasiya Rabchenyuk—none of whom have been suspected of steroid use—competed in the final of the women's 400 meter hurdles during the 2008 Beijing Olympic games.

Some Long-Lasting Track and Field Records

Women's Sprints

Event	World Record Time	Woman	Country	Year
100 meters	10.49	Florence Griffith Joyner	United States	1988
200 meters	21.34	Florence Griffith Joyner	United States	1988
400 meters	47.60	Marita Koch	East Germany	1985
800 meters	1:53.28	Jarmila Kratochvilova	Czechoslovakia	1983

Men's Field Events

Event	World Record Time	Man	Country	Year
High Jump	2.45 meters	Javier Sotomayor	Cuba	1993
Shot Put	23.12 meters	Randy Barnes	United States	1990
Discus	74.08 meters	Jürgen Schult	East Germany	1986
Hammer	86.74 meters	Yuriy Syedikh	Soviet Union	1986

Sports as Entertainment

Sports fans send mixed messages about anabolic steroid use. They accept anti-steroid rhetoric in principle but ignore it in practice. Most fans admit that they want to witness an extraordinary performance. They sympathize with the athlete's quest to go beyond the limits of human endurance. This desire can conflict with their views about drug-free sport.

For example, a poll in 2004 found 91 percent of Americans supported testing baseball players for steroids. Yet baseball attendance has been steady or rising for the last twenty years. "I haven't seen anything that shows me the customers really care," said one steroid expert. "If you view sports as entertainment, why would you draw a distinction? . . . Using the drugs makes the athletes more entertaining. The ball goes out of the park more often." A former baseball player added, "If you polled the fans, I think they'd tell you, 'I don't care about illegal steroids. I'd rather see a guy hit the ball a mile or throw it 105 miles an hour.'" Barry Bonds added, "We're entertainers. If I can't go out there [to play], and somebody pays $60 for a ticket, and I'm not in the lineup, who gets cheated? Not me."

There is certainly an element of self-serving justification in this line of reasoning. How else would steroid-using athletes explain their violation of the rules of their sport (not to mention the laws of the country)? However, fans themselves are ambivalent. In a 2009 poll, 57 percent of fans said they cared "a lot" if baseball players used steroids compared to only 14 percent who said "not at all." Fifty-seven percent said the Hall of Fame should bar players who have used steroids, a serious issue considering that five of the top twelve home run hitters in history (Bonds, Sosa, McGwire, Palmeiro, and Rodriguez) have been accused of using steroids. However, the high price of baseball tickets concerned fans far more than anabolic steroid use.

Many sports fans are ambivalent about whether steroid use should be banned in sports, but this Baltimore Orioles fan makes his feelings about Rafael Palmeiro's suspension for steroid use perfectly clear.

Americans yearn for heroes. Many people view competitive athletics as an escape from the problems of daily life. They do not want to confront the moral and ethical controversies regarding anabolic steroid use.

Even when steroid use is confirmed, official reporting of the fact depends on political, financial, and legal pressures completely independent of the test results. Sports officials privately admit that drug use among athletes is high but relatively few athletes are ever caught. At the higher levels of sports, drug testing is often done mostly for public relations to protect the image of sport.

The culture surrounding modern American sports is more about winning and providing entertainment than about education and building character. In the middle of a recession, John Calipari received an eight-year contract for almost $32 million to coach the University of Kentucky college basketball team. A large segment of the public might be unhappy with elite sports because they feel they are not watching "natural performances." However, another group of Americans has become equally frustrated with the futility of the anti-steroids crusade and more accepting of steroids as simply part of the game.

Repeal of the Anabolic Steroid Control Act?

Decriminalization of anabolic steroids does not look likely any time in the near future. The legalization of drugs—whether marijuana, cocaine, or anabolic steroids—is a controversial position. What some call "accepting reality," others view as a complete collapse of moral responsibility. However, there is a movement to allow the use of steroids if the user is above a certain age and under the strict direction of a physician.

Supporters of decriminalization have argued that the Anabolic Steroid Control Act disregards scientific reality for symbolic effect. Repeal would reduce the law enforcement costs associated with illegal steroid use. Performance-enhancing drugs are not high on the list of drugs that endanger society. Legalization would also reduce the cost of drug testing and reduce the hypocrisy in sport. It's even possible that it might encourage the safe use of steroids, as some argue has occurred with legal abortion and even legalized medical marijuana.

In addition, direct legal efforts to limit anabolic steroid use have not been a great success. The Anabolic Steroid Control Act has reduced the supply of steroids in the United States. However, it does not seem to have had a major impact on the availability or use of steroids. The domestic black market and a constant supply from abroad have overwhelmed any meaningful enforcement of the act. And like the "war on drugs" in general, the Anabolic Steroid Control Act has had unintended consequences. It has undermined respect for the law and de-emphasized public health and education efforts to reduce demand for steroids. The criminalization of steroids has driven them into a murky underground where they are used in a more dangerous way (e.g., sharing needles, impurities in black market products) than if they were legal. Because steroids are illegal, athletes who acquire them on the black market are reluctant to consult with their physician after they begin using them regularly.

However, the U.S. government's position since the late 1980s has been that the risks of steroid use are too great to allow them to be decriminalized or unregulated. Drug testing is part of normal law enforcement because drug use is illegal and must be controlled to prevent crime, social problems, health issues, and addiction. Based on polls, the government's attitude probably reflects the position of a majority of Americans. One author wrote, "legalizing the performance-enhancing substances is not the answer. Cheating is not relative. . . . Illegally distributing or using steroids . . . is illegal and morally questionable. Sports ought to be about mental and physical hard work and the development of athletic skills."

It's also difficult to see how anabolic steroids could ever really be used "safely." Many people who use steroids have the attitude that if one dose works, then five or ten will work even better. At that point, heavy steroid use once again becomes a public health issue.

Genetic Manipulation

It is possible that the development of technology will eliminate the whole question of anabolic steroid use. In the future, athletes may use genetic enhancement to alter the human body, improve their performances, and treat their injuries. Genetic manipulation technologies present philosophical and ethical challenges that go far beyond sports. The scientific, medical, and moral implications are so complex that there are major dilemmas as to how future gene-related technologies will be used.

Gene therapy is used to treat a human body by altering, re-placing, or adding DNA to a cell's DNA to change a genetic defect. The first successful human gene therapy treatment was performed in 1990. Gene therapy is still a young science but already some progress has been made in treating rare genetic problems such as an immune deficiency disease known as "bubble boy" syndrome. Other promising research involves the treatment of anemia and advanced arthritis. Gene therapy techniques are still experimental and patient safety is a real concern.

Studies have shown that gene therapy might be effective to stimulate muscle growth and cure muscle-wasting diseases. This type of gene "doping" could also be used to give athletes greater speed, strength, or endurance. One professor involved in gene therapy said, "The sorts of things you'd want to do to help make muscle stronger or repair itself better in a diseased or old person would also make a healthy young person's muscles stronger and repair faster."

Coaches and athletes have shown an interest in gene therapy and it is already banned under WADA regulations. Yet it may

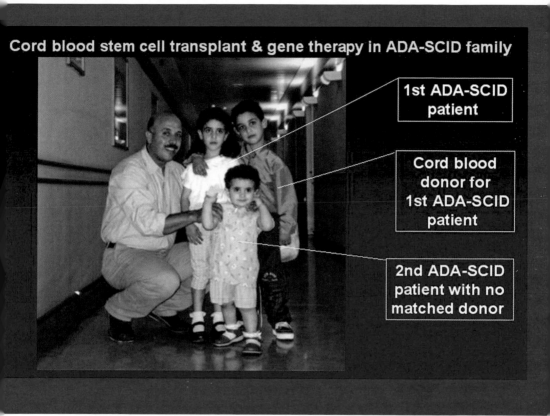

Cord blood stem cell transplant & gene therapy in ADA-SCID family

1st ADA-SCID patient

Cord blood donor for 1st ADA-SCID patient

2nd ADA-SCID patient with no matched donor

Gene therapy may change the whole face of the steroid debate. This two-year-old Israeli Arab girl and her six-year-old sister were born without immune systems, but were cured by gene therapy.

be difficult to create a test that could ever detect gene doping. Any procedure would probably be quite expensive and far too invasive to be medically justified. It would probably be impossible to distinguish DNA created though genetic manipulation from natural DNA.

Genetic engineering might end the controversy over anabolic steroids. However, it will raise new questions. Is it ethical to genetically engineer athletes or breed them as if they were race-horses? Is competing against people with genetically altered bodies "fair"? Is it "cheating" if a less genetically endowed person uses gene doping to "level the playing field"? How will genetically enhanced bodies be distinguished from those enhanced only through training? In the future, what will it mean to be an athlete or to set a record? Will genetic engineering lead to athletes becoming increasingly dehumanized, engineered, and manipulated to provide an entertaining performance?

Winner Take All?

The demand for anabolic steroids in American society is created by the culture's emphasis on winning and physical appearance. People are not born with the desire for a muscular body; it is a value created by society. In the same way, children play games for fun but American society preaches the overriding importance of winning.

Many Americans take a "bottom-line" approach and consider winning the only truly worthwhile goal of competition. If this view is accepted, then it is only a short step to win at all costs. This is the surest way of killing the spirit of play in sport. It reduces the fun of playing and turns the contest into nothing more than a naked power struggle.

The philosophy of "winner take all" makes anabolic steroid use an entirely rational behavior, even if serious side effects are attached to their use. In two national studies, a substantial minority of the anabolic steroids users surveyed expressed no intention of stopping the use of steroids even if negative health effects were definitively proven.

Americans identify very strongly with the small percentage of people who excel, especially in elite sports. The American high jumper John Thomas learned this to his dismay in 1960. Americans expected him to win the gold at the Rome Olympics but Thomas "only" won a bronze medal. Despite being the third best person in the world at his sport, writers and fans turned against him. From this experience, Thomas learned that Americans "only like winners.

They don't give credit to a man for trying. I was called a quitter, a man with no heart." He later added, "American spectators are frustrated athletes. In the champion, they see what they would like to be. In the loser, they see what they actually are, and they treat him with scorn."

American values would have to change if anabolic steroid use is to cease to be a controversial issue. Yet it is almost impossible to change a behavior that has resulted in major benefits for the user, such as improved appearance and athletic performance. For elite athletes, there is also the adulation of fans and media as well as financial, material, and sexual rewards. People would have to be convinced that dishonor is not defeat and ten extra pounds of flab is not a personal tragedy. The anabolic steroid controversy will exist as long as Americans put a higher value on winning than competing, on superficial impressions rather than meaningful values.

Notes

Chapter 1

p. 6: "I'm drug-free . . .": Mark Fainaru-Wada and Lance Williams, "Olympians Got Steroids, Feds Told," *San Francisco Chronicle*, April 25, 2004, www.sfgate.com/cgi-bin/article.cgi?file=/chronicle/archive/2004/04/25/BALCO.TMP (accessed September 13, 2009).

p. 6: "several times . . .": "Disgraced Marion Jones Sentenced to Six Months," National Public Radio, January 11, 2008, www.npr.org/templates/story/story.php?storyId=18028502 (accessed September 13, 2009).

p. 6: "one of the biggest frauds . . .": "Jones Hands Back Olympic Medals," British Broadcasting Company News, October 8, 2007, http://news.bbc.co.uk/sport1/hi/athletics/7034841.stm (accessed September 13, 2009).

p. 10: "Serious sport . . .": D. Eitzen, *Fair and Foul: Beyond the Myths and Paradoxes of Sport*, 3rd ed., Lanham, MD: Rowman and Littlefield, 2006, 51.

p. 10: "I used steroids . . .": Millard Baker, "Arnold Schwarzenegger's Transformation from Steroid User to Anti-Steroid Politician," *Meso-RX Blog*, February 24, 2009, www.mesomorphosis.com/blog/2009/02/24/arnold-schwarzenegger-transformation-from-steroid-user-to-anti-steroid-politician/ (accessed September 14, 2009).

Chapter 2

p. 13: "The testes acts . . .": Charles Yesalis, ed., *Anabolic Steroids in Sport and Exercise*, 2nd ed., Champaign, IL: Human Kinetics, 2000, 19–20.

p. 22: "a government survey . . .": L. D. Johnston, P. M. O'Malley, J. G. Bachman, and J. E. Schulenberg, *Monitoring the Future: National Results on Adolescent Drug Use. Overview of Key Findings, 2007*, Bethesda, MD: National Institute on Drug Abuse, 2007, 42–43.

p. 26: "A survey of Wisconsin high . . .": Joshua Tompkins, "The Creatine Edge," *Los Angeles Times*, May 3, 2004, http://nootropics. com/creatine/athletic.html (accessed September 13, 2009).

p. 27: "Everything I've done . . .": Daniel Rosen, *Dope: A History of Performance Enhancement in Sports from the Nineteenth Century to Today*, Westport, CT: Praeger, 2008, 104–106.

p. 32: "In 2007, a group of scientists . . .": "Scientists Want New Drug Rankings," British Broadcasting Company News, March 23, 2007, http://news.bbc.co.uk/2/hi/health/6474053.stm (accessed September 13, 2009).

Chapter 3

p. 39: "no known chemical agent . . .": Paul Dimeo, *A History of Drug Use in Sport: Beyond Good and Evil*, New York: Routledge, 2007, 92, 18–19.

p. 40: "They identified three conditions that . . .": William Taylor, *Anabolic Steroids and the Athlete*, 2nd ed., Jefferson, NC: McFarland, 2002, 29–34.

p. 43: "In the Tour de France . . .": Jean-Luc van den Broucke, quoted in Eddy Soetaert, "De biecht van Jean-Luc van den Broucke," *Het Volk* [Belgium], October 18, 1978.

p. 46: "For more than a decade . . .": George Mitchell DLA Piper US LLP, "Report to the Commissioner of Baseball of an

Independent Investigation into the Illegal Use of Steroids and Other Performance-enhancing Substances by Players in Major League Baseball," December 13, 2007, http://mlb.mlb.com/mlb/news/mitchell/report.jsp, (accessed September 13, 2009).

p. 55: "Teams draft a kid . . .": Timothy Smith, "N.F.L.'s Steroid Policy Too Lax, Doctor Warns," *New York Times*, July 3, 1991, http://query.nytimes.com/gst/fullpage.html?res=9D0CEEDB1E 3DF930A35754C0A967958260&sec=&spon=&pagewanted=2 (accessed September 13, 2009).

p. 55: "If mature and informed elite athletes . . .": Charles Francis and Jeff Coplon, *Speed Trap: Inside the Biggest Scandal in Olympic History*, New York: St. Martins, 1991.

Chapter 4

p. 58: "Mankind are greater gainers by . . .": John Stuart Mill, *Collected Works*, Vol. 18, *Essays on Politics and Society*, Toronto: University of Toronto Press, 1977, 226, 277, 276–291.

pp. 61–62: "it would not matter . . .": Mark Fainaru-Wada and Lance Williams, *Game of Shadows: Barry Bonds, BALCO, and the Steroids Scandal that Rocked Professional Sports*, New York: Gotham, 2006, 95, 88–104.

p. 68: "special needs . . .": *Walker L. Chandler, et al., Petitioners* v. *Zell D. Miller, Governor of Georgia, et al.*, 520 U.S. 305, 1997, www.law.cornell.edu/supct/html/96-126.ZO.html (accessed September 13, 2009).

p. 68: "public safety . . .": *Chandler* v. *Miller*, 520 U.S. 305, 1997.

pp. 68–69: "virtually any nonconsensual . . .": *Ferguson, et al.* v. *City of Charleston, et al.*, 532 U.S. 67, 2001, www.law.cornell.edu/supct/html/99-936.ZS.html (accessed September 13, 2009).

p. 75: "It can hardly be argued . . .": *Tinker* v. *Des Moines Independent Community School District*, 393 U.S. 503, 1969, www.law.cornell.edu/supct/html/historics/USSC_CR_0393_0503_ZO.html (accessed September 13, 2009).

Chapter 5

p. 78: "successful people do what they . . .": Associated Press, "Lie, Cheat and Steal: High School Ethics Surveyed," *MSNBC. com*, November 30, 2008, www.msnbc.msn.com/id/27983915 (accessed September 13, 2009).

p. 79: "Good grades . . .": David Callahan, "The Cheating Culture," www.cheatingculture.com (accessed September 13, 2009).

p. 79: "If you're not cheating . . .": Michael Schafer and Mary Ann Porucznik, "If You're Not Cheating, You're Not Trying," *AAOS Now*, June 2008, www.aaos.org/news/aaosnow/jun08/cover1.asp (accessed September 13, 2009).

p. 82: "The use of a substance . . .": George Walsh, "Our Drug-happy Athletes," *Sports Illustrated*, November 21, 1960, http://sportsillustrated.cnn.com/vault/article/magazine/ MAG1072027/3/index.htm (accessed September 13, 2009).

p. 82: "Everyone in cycling . . .": Paul Dimeo, *A History of Drug Use in Sport: Beyond Good and Evil*, New York: Routledge, 2007, 60.

p. 83: "We had no reason . . .": Mark Fainaru-Wada and Lance Williams, *Game of Shadows: Barry Bonds, BALCO, and the Steroids Scandal that Rocked Professional Sports*, New York: Gotham, 2006, 187.

p. 83: "At first I felt like a cheater . . .": Tom Verducci, "Steroids in Baseball," *Sports Illustrated*, June 3, 2002, http://sportsillustrated. cnn.com/2004/magazine/03/02/flashback_juiced/index.html (accessed September 14, 2009).

p. 83: "This is not cheating . . .": John McCloskey and Julian Bailes, *When Winning Costs Too Much: Steroids, Supplements, and Scandal in Today's Sports*, New York: Taylor, 2005, 11, 298.

pp. 85–86: "I think it's important . . .": Millard Baker, "Arnold Schwarzenegger's Transformation from Steroid User to Anti-Steroid Politician," *Meso-RX Blog*, February 24, 2009, www.meso-morphosis. com/blog/2009/02/24/arnold-schwarzenegger-transformation-from-steroid-user-to-anti-steroid-politician/ (accessed September 14, 2009).

p. 86: "it is common for famous athletes . . .": George Mitchell DLA Piper US LLP, "Report to the Commissioner of Baseball of an Independent Investigation into the Illegal Use of Steroids and Other Performance-enhancing Substances by Players in Major League Baseball," December 13, 2007, http://mlb.mlb.com/mlb/news/mitchell/report.jsp, (accessed September 13, 2009).

p. 88: "Last year . . .": Charles Yesalis, ed., *Anabolic Steroids in Sport and Exercise*, 2nd ed., Champaign, IL: Human Kinetics, 2000, 55.

p. 92: "comfortable satisfaction": Daniel Rosen, *Dope: A History of Performance Enhancement in Sports from the Nineteenth Century to Today*, Westport, CT: Praeger, 2008, 132–137.

p. 96: "Where an anabolic androgenic . . ."; WADA Code: World Anti-Doping Agency, "The World Anti-Doping Code—The 2009 Prohibited List—International Standard," September 20, 2008, http://74.125.47.132/search?q=cache:wR1gFvGM0oQJ:www.wada-ama.org/rtecontent/document/2009_Prohibited_List_ENG_Final_20_Sept_08.pdf+wada+banned+list&cd=2&hl=en&ct=clnk&gl=us&ie=UTF-8 (accessed September 14, 2009).

p. 99: "Both on a political and juridical level . . .": Lawrence Donegan, "Fifa's Credibility Goes Missing When Drugs Policy is Put to Test," the *Guardian*, March 26, 2009, www.guardian.co.uk/sport/blog/2009/mar/26/lawrence-donegan-football-fifa-wada-doping-drugs (accessed September 14, 2009).

Chapter 6

p. 101: "Illegal steroid use . . .": Mark Fainaru-Wada and Lance Williams, *Game of Shadows: Barry Bonds, BALCO, and the Steroids Scandal that Rocked Professional Sports*, New York: Gotham, 2006, 210.

p. 101: "Let's put the right word on it . . .": Frank Deford, "Clemens' Denial of Steroid Use Hard to Believe," National Public

Radio, January 9, 2008, www.npr.org/templates/story/story.php?storyId=17943759 (accessed September 14, 2009).

p. 102: "about a year or so . . .": Juliet Macur, "Cycling to Use Blood Profiles in Doping Case," *New York Times*, February 27, 2009.

p. 102: "Doping now is everything . . .": "Cycling; A Call for Doping Changes," *New York Times*, July 27, 1998, www.nytimes.com/1998/07/27/sports/cycling-a-call-for-doping-changes.html (accessed September 14, 2009).

p. 104: "It's going to be a dying sport . . .": Fainaru-Wada and Williams, *Game of Shadows*, 19–20.

p. 106: "I haven't seen . . .": Tom Weir, "Drug-free Sports: Do the Fans Care?" *USA Today*, December 8, 2004, www.usatoday.com/sports/2004-12-07-drug-free-sports_x.htm (accessed September 14, 2009).

p. 106: "If you polled the fans..." Tom Verducci, "Steroids in Baseball," *Sports Illustrated*, June 3, 2002, http://sportsillustrated.cnn.com/2004/magazine/03/02/flashback_juiced/index.html (accessed September 14, 2009).

p. 106: "We're entertainers. If I . . .": Barry Bonds quoted in Fainaru-Wada and Williams, *Game of Shadows*, 268.

p. 106: "In a 2009 poll, 57 percent . . .": Ben Walker, "It's a Hit. . . on the Wallet," *Albany Times Union*, April 1, 2009, C:1, 3.

p. 109: "legalizing the performance-enhancing substances . . .": William Boone, *Is Sports Nutrition for Sale?*, New York: Nova Science, 2006, 124.

p. 110: "The sorts of things . . .": Christen Brownlee, "Gene Doping: Will Athletes go for the Ultimate High?" *Science News*, October 30, 2004, http://findarticles.com/p/articles/mi_m1200/is_18_166/ai_n7072715/ (accessed September 14, 2009).

pp. 112–113: "only like winners . . .": Tom Donohue and Neil Johnson, *Foul Play: Drug Abuse in Sports*, New York: Basil Blackwell, 1986, 129, 145.

Further Information

Books

Assael, Shaun. *Steroid Nation: Juiced Home Run Totals, Anti-aging Miracles, and a Hercules in Every High School: The Secret History of America's True Drug Addiction.* New York: ESPN Books, 2007.

Bahrke, Michael, and Charles Yesalis. *Performance-Enhancing Substances in Sport and Exercise.* Champaign, IL: Human Kinetics, 2002.

Beamish, Rob, and Ian Ritchie. *Fastest, Highest, Strongest: A Critique of High-Performance Sport.* New York: Routledge, 2006.

Burns, Christopher, ed. *Doping in Sports.* New York: Nova Science, 2006.

Levert, Suzanne. *The Facts About Steroids.* Tarrytown, NY: Marshall Cavendish, 2004.

Rosen, Daniel. *Dope: A History of Performance Enhancement in Sports from the Nineteenth Century to Today.* Westport, CT: Praeger, 2008.

Soek, Janwillem. *The Strict Liability Principle and the Human Rights of Athletes in Doping Cases.* Cambridge: Cambridge University Press, 2006.

Websites

MayoClinic.com

"Performance-Enhancing Drugs and Your Teen Athlete"

www.mayoclinic.com/print/performance-enhancing-drugs/
SM00045/METHOD=print

National Institute on Drug Abuse (NIDA)

"NIDA for Teens: Anabolic Steroids"

http://teens.drugabuse.gov/drnida/drnida_ster1.php

Open Directory Project

"Sports: Strength Sports: Bodybuilding: Supplements: Anabolic
Steroids"

www.dmoz.org/Sports/Strength_Sports/Bodybuilding/
Supplements/Anabolic_Steroids/

Steroid Nation (On-line journal)

http://grg51.typepad.com/steroid_nation/

U.S. Anti-Doping Agency (USADA)

www.usantidoping.org/

U.S. Drug Enforcement Agency (USDEA)

"Steroid News Releases"

www.usdoj.gov/dea/pubs/pressrel/steroid_index.html

World Anti-Doping Agency (WADA)

www.wada-ama.org/en/index.ch2

Bibliography

"A Level Playing Field?" *Nature*, August 7, 2008, www.nature.com/nature/journal/v454/n7205/full/454667a.html (accessed October 22, 2009).

"Alcohol and Public Health." Centers for Disease Control and Prevention, September 3, 2008, www.cdc.gov/alcohol/ (accessed October 22, 2009).

Anderson, William, and Candice Jackson. "Putting Stars Behind Bars: How Did Breaking Sports Rules Become a Federal Offense?" *Reason*, April 2009, www.reason.com/news/show/131973.html (accessed October 22, 2009).

"Are Anabolic Steroids Addictive? Animal Study Suggests They Are." *Medical News Today*, December 13, 2005, www.medicalnewstoday.com/articles/34928.php (accessed October 22, 2009).

Associated Press. "Calipari Accepts Kentucky's Offer." NBC Sports, *MSNBC.com*, March 31, 2009, http://nbcsports.msnbc.com/id/29956570/ (accessed October 22, 2009).

———. "French Collect Lance's Hair in Test." *ESPN.com*, March 18, 2009, http://sports.espn.go.com/oly/cycling/news/story?id=3992009 (accessed October 22, 2009).

_____. "Greek Sprinters' Trial on Hold." *Sports Illustrated*, February 5, 2009, http://sportsillustrated.cnn.com/2009more/02/05/greece.doping.trial.ap/index.html (accessed October 22, 2009).

_____. "IOC Strips Gold from 2000 Olympics U.S. Relay Team." *ESPN.com*, August 2, 2008, http://sports.espn.go.com/espn/wire?section=oly&id=3515911 (accessed October 22, 2009).

_____. "Lie, Cheat and Steal: High School Ethics Surveyed." *MSNBC.com*, November 30, 2008, www.msnbc.msn.com/id/27983915 (accessed September 13, 2009).

_____. "N.H.L. Says Steroid Use Isn't a Problem among Hockey Players." *ESPN.com*, December 14, 2007, http://sports.espn.go.com/nhl/news/story?id=3155305(accessed October 22, 2009).

Bahrke, Michael, and Charles Yesalis, eds. *Performance-Enhancing Substances in Sport and Exercise.* Champaign, IL: Human Kinetics, 2002.

Baker, Millard. "Arnold Schwarzenegger's Transformation from Steroid User to Anti-Steroid Politician." *Meso-RX Blog*, February 24, 2009, www.mesomorphosis.com/blog/2009/02/24/arnoldsch warzenegger-transformation-from-steroid-user-to-anti-steroid-politician/ (accessed October 22, 2009).

Barnes, J. *A Pack of Lies: Towards a Sociology of Lying.* Cambridge: Cambridge University Press, 1994.

"Baseball Star Rodriguez Confesses Taking Steroids to ESPN." *American Free Press*, February 9, 2008, www.google.com/hosted news/afp/article/ALeqM5hrnuOY5MQ7Zle4f_BtfQqEh8Uafw (accessed October 22, 2009).

"Bettman Testifies NHL is Steroid-free." Canadian Broadcasting Corporation, February 27, 2008, www.cbc.ca/sports/hockey/story/2008/02/27/gary-bettman.html (accessed October 22, 2009).

Board of Education of Independent School District No. 92 of Pottawatomie County v. *Earls.* 536 U.S. 822 (10th Cir. 01-332). 2002, http://caselaw.lp.findlaw.com/scripts/getcase.pl?court=US&vol=000&invol=01-332 (accessed October 22, 2009).

"Bonds' Perjury Trial Delayed Well into Summer." *SI.com,* March 2, 2009, http://sportsillustrated.cnn.com/2009/baseball/mlb/03/02/bonds.delay.ap/index.html (accessed October 22, 2009).

Boone, William. *Is Sports Nutrition for Sale?* New York: Nova Science, 2006.

Brownlee, Christen. "Gene Doping: Will Athletes Go for the Ultimate High?" *Science News,* October 30, 2004, http://findarticles.com/p/articles/mi_m1200/is_18_166/ai_n7072715/ (accessed October 22, 2009).

Callahan, David. "The Cheating Culture." *The Cheating Culture,* www.cheatingculture.com (accessed October 22, 2009).

_____. *The Cheating Culture: Why More Americans Are Doing Wrong to Get Ahead.* New York: Harcourt, 2004.

Canseco, Jose. *Juiced: Wild Times, Rampant 'Roids, Smash Hits, and How Baseball Got Big.* New York: Regan Books, 2005.

_____. *Vindicated: Big Names, Big Liars, and the Battle to Save Baseball.* New York: Simon Spotlight, 2008.

Carroll, Will. *The Juice: The Real Story of Baseball's Drug Problems.* Chicago: Ivan Dee, 2005.

Chambers, Dwain. *Race Against Me: My Story.* Morpeth, United Kingdom: Libros International, 2009.

Chandler v. *Miller.* 520 U.S. 305. 1997, www.law.cornell.edu/supct/html/96-126.ZO.html (accessed October 22, 2009).

"Chargers' Merriman Apologizes, Will Appeal Suspension." *ESPN. com*, October 25, 2006, http://sports.espn.go.com/nfl/news/story?id=2636523 (accessed October 22, 2009).

Charniga, Andrew Jr. "The Effect of Testing for Performance-Enhancing Drugs on the Progress of World Records in Weight-lifting." *Sportivny Press*, 2001, www.dynamic-eleiko.com/sportivny/library/farticles006.html (accessed October 22, 2009).

Coakley, Jay. *Sports in Society: Issues and Controversies.* 8th ed. New York: McGraw Hill, 2004.

Collins, Rick. "The Anabolic Steroid Control Act: The Wrong Prescription." Reprinted with modifications, New York State Bar Association, *Criminal Justice Journal* 9, Summer 2001, *Meso-RX Blog*, http://mesomorphosis.com/articles/collins/wrong-prescription.htm (accessed October 22, 2009).

"Corticosteroids: What Are Those?" *Spirit of Sport*, July–September 2008, 5–6 www.usantidoping.org/files/active/athletes/newsletter/3rd%20qtr%202008%20for%20website.pdf (accessed October 22, 2009).

Cox, Patrick. "Pumping Up Steroid Hysteria." *Meso-RX Blog*, February 11, 2009, www.mesomorphosis.com/articles/cox/steroid-hysteria.htm (accessed October 22, 2009).

"Creatine." *Mayoclinic.com*, www.mayoclinic.com/health/creatine/NS_patient-creatine (accessed October 22, 2009).

"Cycling: A Call for Doping Changes." *New York Times*, July 27, 1998, www.nytimes.com/1998/07/27/sports/cycling-a-call-for-doping-changes.html (accessed October 22, 2009).

Deford, Frank. "Clemens' Denial of Steroid Use Hard to Believe." National Public Radio, January 9, 2008, www.npr.org/templates/story/story.php?storyId=17943759 (accessed October 22, 2009).

Dimeo, Paul. *A History of Drug Use in Sport: Beyond Good and Evil*. New York: Routledge, 2007.

Di Pasquale, Mauro. "Nandrolone Positive Drug Tests—What Do They Mean?" *Think Muscle*, 2004, www.thinkmuscle.com/ARTICLES/dipasquale/nandrolone-positive-drug-tests.htm (accessed October 22, 2009).

Donegan, Lawrence. "Fifa's Credibility Goes Missing When Drugs Policy is Put to Test." the *Guardian*, March 26, 2009, www.guardian.co.uk/sport/blog/2009/mar/26/lawrence-donegan-football-fifa-wada-doping-drugs (accessed October 22, 2009).

Donohue, Tom, and Neil Johnson. *Foul Play: Drug Abuse in Sports*. New York: Basil Blackwell, 1986.

"Doping Scandals Once Again Overshadow Olympic Weightlifting Competition." *International Herald Tribune*, July 13, 2008, www.iht.com/articles/ap/2008/07/12/sports/EU-OLY-WEI-China-Weightlifting-Preview.php (accessed October 22, 2009).

Drewe, Sheryle. *A Philosophical Inquiry into Physical Education and Sports*. Lanham, MD: University Press of America, 2001.

Eggers, Kerry. "NCAA Athletes on the Juice? Local Former Lineman Alleges Steroids Prevalent in College Football." *Portland Tribune*, April 14, 2005, www.portlandtribune.com/sports/story.php?story_id=29338 (accessed October 22, 2009).

Eitzen, D. Stanley. *Fair and Foul: Beyond the Myths and Paradoxes of Sport.* 3rd ed. Lanham, MD: Rowman and Littlefield, 2006.

Fainaru-Wada, Mark, and Lance Williams. *Game of Shadows: Barry Bonds, BALCO, and the Steroids Scandal that Rocked Professional Sports.* New York: Gotham, 2006.

_____."Olympians Got Steroids, Feds Told." *San Francisco Chronicle*, April 25, 2004, www.sfgate.com/cgi-bin/article.cgi?file=/chronicle/archive/2004/04/25/BALCO.TMP (accessed October 22, 2009).

Feezell, Randolph. *Sport, Play, and Ethical Reflection.* Urbana: University of Illinois Press, 2004.

Ferguson v. *Charleston.* 536 U.S. 67. 2001, www.law.cornell.edu/supct/html/99-936.ZS.html (accessed October 22, 2009).

"Focus Attention upon Distributors of Human Growth Hormone, Scientists Urge." *Science Daily,* June 18, 2008, www.sciencedaily.com/releases/2008/06/080617160837.htm (accessed October 22, 2009).

Fraleigh, W. "Performance-Enhancing Drugs in Sport: The Ethical Issue." *Journal of the Philosophy of Sport* 11 (1985): 23–29.

Francis, Charles, and Jeff Coplon. *Speed Trap: Inside the Biggest Scandal in Olympic History.* New York: St. Martins, 1991.

French, Peter. *Ethics and College Sports: Ethics, Sports, and the University.* Lanham, MD: Rowman and Littlefield, 2004.

Fulford, Robert. "Henry Newboldt." *Globe and Mail,* Toronto, Canada, January 7, 1998, www.robertfulford.com/newbolt.html (accessed October 22, 2009).

Gaffney, Gary. "Darrius Miles-NBA Player Inactive for Two Years-Would Be Suspended Ten Games in Comeback." *Steroid Nation,* December 14, 2008, http://grg51.typepad.com/steroid_nation/2008/12/darrius-miles-.html (accessed October 22, 2009).

Gallagher, Brendan. "Tom Simpson Haunts Tour 40 Years On." *Telegraph,* 3 August 2007, www.telegraph.co.uk/sport/columnists/brendangallagher/2316933/Tom-Simpson-haunts-Tour-40-years-on.html (accessed October 22, 2009).

Gardner, R. "On Performance-Enhancing Substances and the Unfair Advantage Argument." *Journal of the Philosophy of Sport* 16 (1989): 59–83.

Gay, Nancy. "Steroids Spotlight Turns to Football." *San Francisco Chronicle,* October 27, 2006, www.sfgate.com/cgi-bin/article.cgi?f=/c/a/2006/10/27/SPG9AM0RPD1.DTL (accessed October 22, 2009).

Goldman, Tom. "Disgraced Marion Jones Sentenced to Six Months." National Public Radio, January 11, 2008, www.npr.org/templates/story/story.php?storyId=18028502 (accessed October 22, 2009).

Graham, M.R., et al. "Anabolic Steroid Use: Patterns of Use and Detection of Doping." *Sports Medicine* 38 (2008): 505–525.

Greene, Lisa, and Dave Scheiber. "'Roid Rage." *St. Petersburg Times,* February 21, 2005, www.sptimes.com/2005/02/21/Sports/_Roid_rage.shtml (accessed October 22, 2009).

Hellerman, Caleb. "Human Growth Hormone Use Rises, but Is It Legal?" *CNN.com*, May 9, 2007, www.cnn.com/2007/HEALTH/04/11/chasing.hgh/ (accessed October 22, 2009).

Hoberman, John. *Testosterone Dreams: Rejuvenation, Aphrodisia, Doping.* Berkeley: University of California Press, 2006.

Huizinga, Johan. *Homo Ludens: A Study of the Play Element in Culture.* Boston: Beacon Press, 1950.

Jenkins, Mark. "Creatine Supplementation in Athletes: Review." *SportsMed Web,* 1998, www.rice.edu/~jenky/sports/creatine.html (accessed October 22, 2009).

Johnston, L. D., P. M. O'Malley, J. G. Bachman, and J. E. Schulenberg. *Monitoring the Future: National Results on Adolescent Drug Use. Overview of Key Findings, 2007.* Bethesda, MD: National Institute on Drug Abuse, 2007, http://monitoringthefuture.org/new.html (accessed October 22, 2009).

_____. *Monitoring the Future: National Survey Results on Drug Use, 1975-2006: Volume II, College Students and Adults Ages 19-45. Overview of Key Findings, 2007.* Bethesda, MD: National Institute on Drug Abuse, 2006, http://monitoringthefuture.org/new.html (accessed October 22, 2009).

"Jones Hands Back Olympic Medals." British Broadcasting Company News, October 8, 2007, http://news.bbc.co.uk/sport1/hi/athletics/7034841.stm (accessed September 13, 2009).

Kious, B. "Philosophy on Steroids: Why the Anti-doping Position Could Use a Little Enhancement." *Theoretical Medicine and Bioethics* 29 (2008): 213–234.

Koerner, Brendan. "Where Do Athletes Go to Court." *Slate*, July 1, 2004, www.slate.com/Default.aspx?id=2103285 (accessed October 22, 2009).

Landis, Floyd, and Loren Mooney. *Positively False: The Real Story of How I Won the Tour de France*. New York: Simon Spotlight Entertainment, 2007.

Lenehan, Pat. *Anabolic Steroids and Other Performance-enhancing Drugs*. London: Taylor and Francis, 2003.

Lipsyte, Robert. "BackTalk: Steroids Raise Fuss and Muscles." *New York Times*, June 23, 2002.

Livingstone, Seth. "Fight against Steroids Gaining Muscle in High School Athletics." *USA Today*, June 8, 2005, www.usatoday.com/sports/preps/2005-06-08-sports-weekly-steroids-report_x.htm (accessed October 22, 2009).

Macur, Juliet. "Cycling to Use Blood Profiles in Doping Case." *New York Times*, February 27, 2009.

May, Paul. "Nandrolone." *Molecule of the Month*, University of Bristol, October 2000, www.chm.bris.ac.uk/motm/nandrolone/nandh.htm (accessed October 22, 2009).

McCaig, Sam. "NHL Can't Ignore Steroid Issue." *Hockey News*, December 14, 2007, www.thehockeynews.com/articles/11933-From-The-Point-NHL-cant-ignore-steriod-issue.html (accessed October 22, 2009).

McCloskey, John, and Julian Bailes. *When Winning Costs Too Much: Steroids, Supplements, and Scandal in Today's Sports*. New York: Taylor Trade, 2005.

McNamee, M., and S. Parry, eds. *Ethics and Sport.* London: Rout-ledge, 1998.

Miah, Andy. *Genetically Modified Athletes: Biomedical Ethics, Gene Doping, and Sport.* London: Routledge, 2004.

Mill, John Stuart. *Collected Works.* Vol. 18, *Essays on Politics and Society.* Toronto: University of Toronto Press, 1977.

Mitchell, George, DLA Piper US LLP. "Report to the Commissioner of Baseball of an Independent Investigation into the Illegal Use of Steroids and Other Performance-enhancing Substances by Players in Major League Baseball." December 13, 2007, http://mlb.mlb.com/mlb/news/mitchell/report.jsp (accessed September 13, 2009).

Mitchell, Robert, and Nicholas Thompson, eds. *Deception: Perspectives on Human and Nonhuman Deceit.* Albany: SUNY Press, 1986.

Moller, Vernon. "Knud Enemark Jensen's Death during the 1960 Rome Olympics: A Search for Truth?" *Sport in History* 25 (December 2005): 452–471.

Mortenson, Chris. "Chargers LB Tested Clean 19 of 20 Times." *ESPN.com,* April 30, 2007, http://sports.espn.go.com/nfl/news/story?id=2853277 (accessed October 27, 2009).

Mulvaney, Kieran. "Boxing Does Not Escape the Specter of Steroids." *ESPN.com,* March 1, 2007, http://sports.espn.go.com/sports/boxing/news/story?id=2782402 (accessed October 22, 2009).

National Basketball Player's Association. "Article XXXIII-Anti-Drug Program." *Collective Bargaining Agreement,* www.nbpa.com/cba_articles/article-XXXIII.php#section9 (accessed October 22, 2009).

National Institute on Drug Abuse [NIDA]. "NIDA InfoFacts: Steroids (Anabolic-Androgenic)." National Institutes of Health, July 2009, www.nida.nih.gov/infofacts/steroids.html (accessed October 22, 2009).

National Institutes of Health. *Anabolic Steroids.* Bethesda, MD: National Institute on Drug Abuse, 2000.

National Treasury Employees Union v. *Von Raab.* 498 U.S. 656. 1989, http://supreme.justia.com/us/489/656/case.html (accessed October 22, 2009).

Natural Products Association. "Industry Facts [2006]." www.naturalproductsassoc.org/site/PageServer?pagename=ln_NNFA IndustryFacts (accessed October 22, 2009).

"N.F.L. Steroid Policy 'Not Perfect.'" CBS News, April 27, 2005, www.cbsnews.com/stories/2005/04/27/national/main691147_page3.shtml (accessed October 22, 2009).

Noble, Holcomb. "Steroid Use by Teen-Age Girls Is Rising." *New York Times*, June 1, 1999.

Pagonis, T. A., N. V. Angelopoulos, G. N. Koukoulis, and C. S. Hadjichristodoulou. "Psychiatric Side Effects Induced by Supraphysiological Doses of Combinations of Anabolic Steroids Correlate to the Severity of Abuse." *European Psychiatry* 8 (December 21, 2006): 563–569.

Perry, Dayn. "Pumped-Up Hysteria: Forget the Hype. Steroids Aren't Wrecking Professional Baseball." *Reason*, January 2003, www.reason.com/news/show/28645.html (accessed October 22, 2009).

Prettyman, Sandra, and Brian Lampman, eds. *Learning Culture through Sports*. Lanham, MD: Rowman and Littlefield, 2006.

Roberts, Selena, and David Epstein. "Sources Tell *SI* Alex Rodriguez Tested Positive for Steroids in 2003." *Sports Illustrated*, February 7, 2009, http://sportsillustrated.cnn.com/2009/baseball/mlb/02/07/alex-rodriguez-steroids/.

Rosen, Daniel. *Dope: A History of Performance Enhancement in Sports from the Nineteenth Century to Today*. Westport, CT: Praeger, 2008.

Schafer, Michael, and Mary Ann Porucznik. "If You're Not Cheating, You're Not Trying." *AAOS Now*, June 2008, www.aaos.org/news/aaosnow/jun08/cover1.asp (accessed October 22, 2009).

Schmidt, Michael. "Clemens's Ex-Trainer to Meet with Prosecutors." *New York Times*, January 12, 2009.

Schneider, Angela, and Theodore Friedmann. *Gene Doping in Sports: The Science and Ethics of Genetically Modified Athletes*. Boston: Elsevier, 2006.

Schwarz, Alan, and Michael Schmidt. "Clemens Says Injections Were Not Steroids." *New York Times*, January 4, 2008, www.nytimes.com/2008/01/04/sports/baseball/04clemens.html (accessed October 22, 2009).

"Scientists Want New Drug Rankings." British Broadcasting Company News, March 23, 2007, http://news.bbc.co.uk/2/hi/health/6474053.stm (accessed October 22, 2009).

Simon, Robert L. *Fair Play: The Ethics of Sport*. 2nd ed. Boulder, CO: Westview Press, 2004.

_____. "Good Competition and Drug-Enhanced Performance." *Journal of the Philosophy of Sport* 11 (1984): 6–13.

Sjöqvist, F., M. Garle, and A. Rane. "Use of Doping Agents, Particularly Anabolic "Smoking and Tobacco Use." Centers for Disease Control and Prevention. January 2008, www.cdc.gov/tobacco/Data_statistics/fact_sheets/health_effects/health_effects.htm (accessed October 22, 2009).

Slater, Matt. "Berlin Panned for Chambers Invite." British Broadcasting Company News, March 12, 2009, http://news.bbc.co.uk/sport1/hi/athletics/7938590.stm (accessed October 22, 2009).

Smith, Timothy. "N.F.L.'s Steroid Policy Too Lax, Doctor Warns." *New York Times*, July 3, 1991, http://query.nytimes.com/gst/fullpage.html?res=9D0CEEDB1E3DF930A35754C0A967958260&sec=&spon=&pagewanted=2 (accessed October 22, 2009).

"Sprinter Collins Reinstated." *Daily Telegraph*, Australia, May 15, 2008, www.news.com.au/dailytelegraph/story/0,22049,23702426-5014066,00.html (accessed October 22, 2009).

"Steroids." Australian Institute of Criminology. March 5, 2009, www.aic.gov.au/research/drugs/types/steroids.html (accessed October 22, 2009).

"Steroids, in Sports and Society." *Lancet*. May 31, 2008: 1872–1882.

Taylor, William N. *Anabolic Steroids and the Athlete*. 2nd ed. Jefferson, NC: McFarland, 2002.

"The Screening Process: A Guide to Testing Policies, from Pros to High School." *Sports Illustrated*, March 11, 2008, http://sportsillustrated.cnn.com/2008/magazine/03/11/steroid.testing policies/index.html (accessed October 22, 2009).

Tinker v. *Des Moines Independent Community School District.* 393 U.S. 503. 1969, www.law.cornell.edu/supct/html/historics/USSC_CR_0393_0503_ZO.html (accessed October 22, 2009).

Tompkins, Joshua. "The Creatine Edge." *Los Angeles Times*, May 3, 2004, http://nootropics.com/creatine/athletic.html (accessed October 22, 2009).

Ungerleider, Steven. *Faust's Gold: Inside the East German Doping Machine.* New York: St. Martin's Press, 2001.

"Upshaw Tells Newspaper He Doubts WADA's Credibility." *ESPN.com*, http://sports.espn.go.com/nfl/news/story?id=2738172 (accessed October 22, 2009).

U.S. Anti-Doping Agency. "Steroids: The Health Risks." *Spirit of Sport*, vol. 6, issue 4, October–December 2006: 4–5, www.usantidoping.org/files/active/athletes/newsletter/4th%20qtr%20to%20web[1][1].pdf (accessed October 22, 2009).

U.S. Drug Enforcement Agency. "Controlled Substances Act [1990]." www.usdoj.gov/dea/pubs/csa.html (accessed October 22, 2009).

_____. "DEA Leads Largest Steroid Bust in History." December 15, 2005, www.usdoj.gov/dea/pubs/pressrel/pr121505.html (accessed October 22, 2009).

_____. "Steroid Abuse in Today's Society." March 2004, www.deadiversion.usdoj.gov/pubs/brochures/steroids/professionals/index.html (accessed October 22, 2009).

_____. "Steroids." www.usdoj.gov/dea/concern/steroids.html (accessed October 22, 2009).

_____. "Twelve Indicted in Nationwide Anabolic Steroids Probe." January 22, 2009, www.usdoj.gov/dea/pubs/states/newsrel/2009/neworleans012209b.html (accessed October 22, 2009).

Verducci, Tom. "Steroids in Baseball." *Sports Illustrated*, June 3, 2002 http://sportsillustrated.cnn.com/2004/magazine/03/02/flashback_juiced/index.html (accessed October 22, 2009).

Vernonia School District 47J v. Wayne Acton. 515 U.S. 646. 1995, http://caselaw.lp.findlaw.com/scripts/getcase.pl?court=US&vol=000&invol=u10263 (accessed October 22, 2009).

Voet, Willy. *Breaking the Chain: Drugs and Cycling, The True Story*. Trans. William Fotheringham. London: Yellow Jersey, 2002.

Walker, Ben. "It's a Hit…on the Wallet." *Albany Times Union*, April 1, 2009, C:1, C:3.

Walsh, George. "Our Drug-happy Athletes." *Sports Illustrated*, November 21, 1960, http://sportsillustrated.cnn.com/vault/article/magazine/MAG1072027/3/index.htm (accessed October 22, 2009).

Weir, Tom. "Drug-free Sports: Do the Fans Care?" *USA Today*, December 8, 2004, www.usatoday.com/sports/2004-12-07-drug-free-sports_x.htm (accessed October 22, 2009).

Williams, Lance. "HGH Test Not Catching Users." *San Francisco Chronicle*, November 11, 2008, www.sfgate.com/cgi-bin/article.cgi?f=/c/a/2008/11/10/SP8M141JOG.DTL (accessed October 22, 2009).

Wilson, Duff, and Michael Schmidt. "Steroid Report Cites 'Collective Failure.'" *New York Times*, December 14, 2007.

Wilson, Wayne, and Edward Derse, eds. *Doping in Elite Sport: The Politics of Drugs in the Olympic Movement.* Champaign, IL: Human Kinetics, 2001.

"Women's World Records, Track and Field." *Track and Field News,* 2004, www.trackandfieldnews.com/tfn/records/records.jsp?sex=W&typeId=0&listId=2 (accessed October 22, 2009).

World Anti-Doping Agency. "The World Anti-Doping Code—The 2008 Prohibited List—International Standard." January 2008, www.wada-ama.org/rtecontent/document/2008_List_En.pdf+wada+2008+prohibited+list&hl=en&ct=clnk&cd=1&gl=us&ie=UTF-8 (accessed October 22, 2009).

Yesalis, Charles, ed. *Anabolic Steroids in Sport and Exercise.* 2nd ed. Champaign, IL: Human Kinetics, 2000.

Yost, Pete. "DEA Announces Wide-Ranging Steroid Busts." *Deseret News,* Salt Lake City, September 24, 2007, http://findarticles.com/p/articles/mi_qn4188/is_20070924/ai_n20519121/pg_ (accessed October 22, 2009).

Index

Page numbers in **boldface** are illustrations, tables, and charts.

About the Author

JON STERNGASS is a freelance writer specializing in children's nonfiction books. He has written more than forty books; his recent works include biographies of Jerry Rice, Frederick Douglass, and Geronimo, and a history of Filipino Americans. Born and raised in Brooklyn, Jon Sterngass has a B.A. from Franklin and Marshall College, an M.A. in medieval history from the University of Wisconsin-Milwaukee, and a Ph.D. from City University of New York in nineteenth-century American history. He has lived in Saratoga Springs, New York, for seventeen years with his wife, Karen Weltman, and sons Eli and Aaron. He has been fascinated by the issue of performance-enhancing drugs in sports since Ben Johnson's fall from grace in the 1988 Olympics. *Steroids* is his first book for Marshall Cavendish Benchmark.